MW00583543

Benjamin S. Bloom

Portraits of an Educator

Second Edition

Edited by Thomas R. Guskey

ROWMAN & LITTLEFIELD EDUCATION
A division of
ROWMAN & LITTLEFIELD PUBLISHERS, INC.
Lanham • New York • Toronto • Plymouth, UK

WITHDRAWN
UTSA Libraries

Published by Rowman & Littlefield Education
A division of Rowman & Littlefield Publishers, Inc.
A wholly owned subsidiary of The Rowman & Littlefield Publishing Group, Inc.
4501 Forbes Boulevard, Suite 200, Lanham, Maryland 20706
www.rowman.com

10 Thornbury Road, Plymouth PL6 7PP, United Kingdom

Copyright © 2012 by Thomas R. Guskey

All rights reserved. No part of this book may be reproduced in any form or by any electronic or mechanical means, including information storage and retrieval systems, without written permission from the publisher, except by a reviewer who may quote passages in a review.

British Library Cataloguing in Publication Information Available

Library of Congress Cataloging-in-Publication Data

Benjamin S. Bloom : portraits of an educator / [edited by]Thomas R. Guskey.—2nd ed.
    p. cm.
  Includes bibliographical references.
  ISBN 978-1-61048-603-3 (cloth : alk. paper)—ISBN 978-1-61048-604-0 (pbk. : alk. paper)—ISBN 978-1-61048-605-7 (ebook)
  1. Bloom, Benjamin Samuel, 1913– 2. Educators—United States—Biography. I. Guskey, Thomas R. II. Title.
  LA2317.B545B46 2012
  370.92—dc23
  [B]   2011044669

∞ ™ The paper used in this publication meets the minimum requirements of American National Standard for Information Sciences—Permanence of Paper for Printed Library Materials, ANSI/NISO Z39.48-1992.

Printed in the United States of America

Library
University of Texas
at San Antonio

Contents

Foreword
by Jonathan E. Bloom

I was pleasantly surprised when my brother, David, suggested that we collaborate on a foreword for the revised edition of Professor Thomas R. Guskey's book, *Benjamin S. Bloom: Portraits of an Educator*. Upon rereading the book, it struck me again that Professor Guskey had assembled a compilation of exceptional remembrances of my father, Benjamin S. Bloom. To be consistent with the spirit and the structure of the book I decided that rather than collaborating, we should contribute our individual, unique memories of Dad.

That said, Dad often worked with other writers. His deeply held belief was that each idea, each chapter, and ultimately the entire work would stand or fall on its merits.

When I was about six or seven years old, Dad had a consulting job in Pennsylvania. He asked me if I would like to go with him on the trip. I immediately said yes. I was thrilled to take a business trip with Dad—just the two of us. We boarded the train, and I was amazed that we had our very own private compartment. I remember asking Dad where we would sleep. With a twinkle in his eye, he said that he was not sure, but perhaps "here" and he yanked the bed out of the wall. I was shocked that a bed could be hidden in the wall. Dad just chuckled. As the train rolled into Pennsylvania, he pointed to places where he had worked, gone to school, and showed me the Horseshoe Curve at Altoona where you could see both the beginning and the end of the train.

We ate in the dining car. Dad, who at that time did not earn a great deal of money, made it seem as though there were no limits. It was an experience that was very important to him and was and is imbedded into my memories. As evidenced in his words and his actions, Dad was a most generous soul, and a deeply humble and loving father.

One of my fondest remembrances was lunch at the Quadrangle Club on the University of Chicago campus. Dad had a particular table that he liked near the back of the dining room along the wall. I was probably eight or nine years old when we had our first lunch together. I remember sitting across from Dad and looking at the menu. Being very unsure of what to order, I asked Dad what he thought that I should eat. He replied, "Order anything that you want and I will write it on the check." I meekly asked for a ham sandwich. My father burst out laughing. At the time he did not tell me what he thought was so funny and as promised, whatever I wanted, I had my ham sandwich. Later Dad nearly caused an automobile collision when he told the story to Mom's orthodox Jewish relatives.

We had many lunches over the years at the Quadrangle Club. I treasure the memories of each and every one. They were as important to Dad as they were to me. He often talked about his current work, drawing statistical graphs on the napkins (his blackboard was back in his office).

At Dad's funeral, one of his students told me that Dad would drop everything to have lunch with either of his sons, which the student believed evidenced his great love for his children. I agree. And I want to add that this great love was what drove him for his entire life, permeating every aspect of who he was and what he did.

It is beyond my limited capabilities to adequately capture the man who was Benjamin Samuel Bloom. He was a complete scholar, voracious reader, worked harder than most, prolific writer, and was an unusual and wonderful father and friend.

In his acknowledgments, Professor Guskey writes, "We will never be able to repay all that he did for us, and he never would have expected that." Dad was demanding, but for those that put in the work he would move heaven and earth to provide support. He believed that the reward for a great teacher is the student that eventually surpasses the teacher.

December 2010
Jonathan Bloom is the elder son of Benjamin and Sophie Bloom.

Foreword
by David Bloom

My father had an extraordinary sense of the power of the right question asked at the right time. This was apparent in his field but perhaps not as well known in all the other areas where his incisive questions stimulated new ideas and perspectives. He had an unusual curiosity for the unknown and the intelligence and imagination to ask probing questions. Where most wouldn't even know enough to ask, his interest in people and the world compelled him to pose the most penetrating questions. His queries ranged from very practical to thought provoking and paradigm changing. He could see both material and ideal relationships that few would notice. His ability to communicate complex problems in understandable ways made him the ultimate teacher, one who could teach people from all over the world regardless of their backgrounds. In his work with educators and students, as with his relatives and friends, he was the personification of a better future.

When I was about eight my father built a little roller coaster for my brother and me in our basement. He liked to make things and wanted to give his kids a thrill. But even more, he knew that the roller coaster would draw other kids to the house. Right after the roller coaster was built I started my own club, the Secret Service. Part of my impetus was the magnetic pull of the roller coaster. My father always wanted me to lead and to make things happen, and this was the beginning.

He had a light, friendly presence in his many interactions, always treating everyone with respect. He would never belittle anyone or try to deprive them of their pride. But he didn't have much patience for sloppy thinking, treating it like it was the opposite of a better future.

When he had been sick with Alzheimer's for many years, I would take him out to lunch and he would talk to total strangers as if they were lifelong friends. It was as if he were telling each person he encountered that they were necessary and important. For him the world wasn't something he feared; it was an endless source of interesting potential and possibilities.

I remember once my family had just sat down for dinner when we heard a scream coming from the street. Without hesitating, my father bolted out the door and ran down the street to aid a woman whose purse had been stolen. Fortunately for her, two high school track stars happened to be walking down the street and they caught the thief and retrieved her purse. My father had no concern for his own safety, but an instinctive impulse to help someone in need. This event and so many others showed me my father's deep and abiding connection to the world, both in the way he lived his daily life and in his devotion to improving the lives of others.

June 2011
David Bloom is the younger son of Benjamin and Sophie Bloom.

Preface

Thomas R. Guskey

To be possessed of a vigorous mind is not enough; the prime requisite
is rightly to apply it.

—Rene Descartes

Every field has its giants—individuals whose influence and accomplishments stand far above those of others. When we think of music, for instance, Beethoven and Mozart immediately come to mind. In physics we have Bohr, Currie, and Einstein. In art we think of Rembrandt, Van Gogh, and Picasso. These incredible individuals applied their vigorous minds in extraordinary ways. Their view of the world was completely unique, and they approached their work differently than did anyone before them. Their inimitable insights brought new understandings and groundbreaking advances. They transformed their respective fields in significant and fundamental ways. Even today, in some cases centuries later, we remain awed by their brilliance and the tremendous impact of their work. In education, perhaps no one's work over the last century better fits this description than that of Benjamin S. Bloom.

During a professional career that spanned five decades, Benjamin Bloom produced some of the most important and most influential works in education. Beginning in the 1940s he created new ways to study students' thought processes during instruction and testing in order to encourage the development of more complex reasoning and problem-solving skills. In the 1950s he led efforts to build a framework for classifying instructional goals and assessment questions that became the foundation for curriculum reform worldwide. During the 1960s his explorations of environmental influences on child development provided the foundation for Head Start and other early childhood education programs. Then in the 1970s he outlined procedures for improving the quality of classroom instruction so that virtually all students could reach very high levels of achievement. Coinciding with this work he initiated a collaborative, international effort to establish curriculum centers in nations throughout the world where information on student achievement could be collected, analyzed, and compared. Finally in the 1980s he launched a major project to understand better how individuals develop extraordinary levels of intellectual, artistic, and athletic talent.

Because much his work emphasized educators' unrealized potential to help all students achieve at high levels, some considered Benjamin Bloom an overly optimistic idealist. But those close to him knew that he despised that label. In fact, he distained irrational optimism and had little patience for wishful thinking. He considered himself instead "a reasoned opportunist." In his work he consistently acknowledged the powerful influence of social, demographic, and economic factors on educational outcomes. But rather than describe what is *typical*, Ben sought to determine what is *possible*. His work focused on factors that educators control and can alter in order to provide highly favorable learning conditions for *all* students. Under these more favorable conditions, he believed that virtually all students could learn well, reach high levels of achievement, and gain the many positive benefits of that success.

Benjamin Bloom's association with the Department of Education at the University of Chicago began in 1940, when he started his doctoral studies and worked as a research assistant for the Board of Examinations. It continued until he retired in 1991 as the Charles H. Swift Distinguished Service Professor. From 1943 to 1959 he served as the College's university examiner. He also founded and chaired the University of Chicago's Measurement, Evaluation, and Statistical Analysis Program, or MESA, the preeminent program in quantitative research and evaluation at the time.

Throughout his career, nations throughout the world sought Ben's services as a consultant. He was educational advisor to the government of India from 1957 to 1959, to the government of Israel in 1963 and 1968, and served as consultant for briefer periods to many other countries. He was a founding member and leader of the International Association for the Evaluation of Educational Achievement (IEA) and of the International Curriculum Association. He also directed the first International Seminar for Advanced Training in Curriculum Development held in Sweden in 1971.

In the United States, Ben served as president of the American Educational Research Association, as chairman of the Research and Development Committees of the College Entrance Examination Board and the National Laboratory on Early Childhood Education, and as a member of the National

Academy of Education. He was recipient of the John Dewey Award from the John Dewey Society, the Teachers College Medal for Distinguished Service from Columbia University, the American Educational Research Association/Phi Delta Kappa Award for Distinguished Contributions to Education, and the American Psychological Association's Thorndike Memorial Award. He authored or co-authored seventeen major books and wrote numerous journal articles, most of which are listed in appendix A of this book. His renown also led to many articles being written about him and his work, and a collection of these are included in appendix B.

During his long career Ben made numerous presentations at educational conferences and seminars around the world. But he was never completely comfortable with large group lectures. He much preferred a more personal, one-to-one exchange. To him, this was clearly the best way to teach and the most effective way to learn. As a result, Ben spent much of his time in one-to-one interactions with students and colleagues, discussing, arguing, teaching, and learning.

From these numerous, highly personal, one-to-one interactions grew a variety of what are affectionately known as "Bloom stories"—tales of special exchanges or personal experiences shared with "Mr. Bloom." These stories compose a rich oral history. They are told and retold whenever his former colleagues and students gather. Some stories have actually gained legendary status.

Many "Bloom stories" are humorous and show Ben's amazing quick wit. Some recall the kindness, encouragement, and wisdom he showed in helping students and colleagues overcome obstacles or setbacks. Others relate to how he expressed his dissatisfaction with students' work that did not aim high enough or was not as good as he believed it could be. Still others provide rare glimpses into his special way of thinking and what he considered to be the moral obligation of educators to improve the lives of students. "If we're not doing that," he often said, "then we're not doing our job." Regardless of their content, however, all of the stories reveal touching remembrances of Ben's uniqueness as a scholar, colleague, mentor, and friend.

This book contains many of those better-known "Bloom stories," including several that were not included in the first edition, accompanied by brief descriptions of some of Ben's major professional contributions. In this second edition, special effort also has been made to show the influence of his work, often unacknowledged, on many of the most current innovations in education. The descriptions of his work provide a contextual framework for the stories and, because of their well-known influence, were relatively easy to put together. Most of Ben's works have been published and reprinted in numerous formats. Gathering the stories, however, proved a more formidable task.

A sad and truly regrettable occurrence took place at the University of Chicago shortly after Ben retired in 1991. A few irresponsible, high-level university administrators failed to support the university's renowned Department of Education and eventually closed it. These uninformed and visionless individuals starved and then destroyed the academic home of John Dewey, Charles Judd, Ralph Tyler, Allison Davis, Ben, and many other of the world's most distinguished education scholars. They brought to an end a department that had served as the model for schools of education throughout the United States and around the world. Their shameful and reprehensible deed also made it difficult for me to obtain records of Ben's students and the colleagues with whom he worked.

Fortunately, with the kind assistance of Ms. Belinda Winans, a former secretary in the Department of Education, I was able to obtain a list of all of the students on whose doctoral committees Ben served. During his years at the University of Chicago from 1942 until 1991, Ben chaired the doctoral dissertation committees of sixty-six students and served as a member of doctoral committees for sixty-nine others. The names of these students, many of whom have gone on to make outstanding contributions of their own, are included in appendixes C and D. Ms. Winans also helped me develop a list of all the faculty members in the Department of Education who were Ben's colleagues during those years. With the cooperation of the Alumni Office at the University of Chicago, I then obtained mailing addresses for these former students and faculty. Ben's wife, Ms. Sophie Bloom, also provided me with the names and addresses of others who were close friends and associates of Ben's outside of the university community.

In 2004 I wrote personal letters to each of these individuals, explaining my project and asking them to send me their stories and remembrances. The response was immediate and quite amazing. Letters poured in from around the world, many from some of the most prominent names in education at the time.

One day, for example, I answered my phone to hear a brusque and distant voice ask, "Tom?"

"Yes," I replied, "this is Tom Guskey."

"This is Torsten Husén from Sweden. I can't talk long. We are on a break from the Nobel Committee. But I wanted to let you know that I received your letter and will be sending you several pieces for your consideration."

Although I had never met Torsten Husén, I knew his name well. At the time, he was one of the most eminent educational researchers and scholars in all of Europe. Torsten and Ben worked together for many years in efforts to develop and sustain the International Association for the Evaluation of Educational Achievement (IEA). And here he was, on a break from making decisions about who would receive the Nobel Peace Prizes, talking to me on the telephone.

Stumbling over my words, I managed to say "Thank you" and something about how I would look forward to receiving his stories. A few weeks later two stories and a brief article arrived by mail from Sweden. Unfortunately for me, all were written in Swedish. With the kind assistance of Judith Monsaas, a former Bloom student and then professor of education at West Georgia College, and Kristina Stroede, program coordinator with the Board of Regents of the University System of Georgia, I was able to have these stories and article translated to include in the book.

The descriptions of Ben's professional work included here are arranged chronologically, beginning with his earliest research and writing. Most of the stories are similarly ordered, but not always. Those that reflect more general observations of Ben as a scholar, mentor, or friend are scattered in no particular order. Although edited for format and consistency, most of the stories remain much as they were written.

Acknowledgments

As is true with any collaborative endeavor, I owe a great deal to the many people who helped me put together both editions of this book. First and foremost, of course, is the person to whom this book is dedicated, Professor Benjamin S. Bloom. It was Ben who drew me to study at the University of Chicago. He served as my advisor during my years as a graduate student there and chaired my doctoral dissertation committee. Following my graduation, we worked together on several research projects that were successful largely due to his wise counsel. To me and to so many others, Ben was a demanding teacher, an understanding mentor, and the truest of friends. We will never be able to repay all that he did for us, and he never would have expected that. This book is our simple way of helping others to understand what he was like, not only as the most eminent educational scholar of his time, but as a person. It is also our modest way of saying, "Thank you!"

In addition to the colleagues, students, friends, and family members of Ben's who provided me with the wonderful stories included in this book, I am particularly indebted to Ben's wife, Ms. Sophie Bloom. Everyone who worked with Ben knows the powerful inspiration she was in his life and in his work. But to those who studied under Ben, Sophie was also a confidant and friend. Many of the letters I received about Ben made special mention of Sophie's kindness, warmth, and generosity—qualities that seemed to have grown even deeper and more evident over the years.

Sophie was a woman of incomparable grace, strength, and compassion. Not only did she provide me with the names and addresses of many of Ben's personal and professional friends, she shared with me many unique insights into Ben's manner, his work, and his professional accomplishments. After a great deal of persuading, I was able to convince her to write the foreword to the first edition of this book. It is included in this edition as chapter 1.

Sophie Bloom passed away in May 2010 at the age of ninety-two. She was a major inspiration for this second edition. Without her kind help and assistance, none of this work would have been possible.

I also owe a great deal to my dear friends, Edward (Skip) Kifer and Lorin W. Anderson. Skip is a former student of Ben's and my colleague at the University of Kentucky. On numerous occasions he offered me new perspectives on aspects of Ben's work and his relationships with professional colleagues during the years before I came to know Ben. Lorin, emeritus professor of education at the University of South Carolina and also a former student of Ben's, wrote several superb articles on Ben's work that proved particularly helpful in putting this book together. He also advised me on the book's development and provided me with many valuable suggestions. Much of what is included on these pages reflects Skip's and Lorin's ideas.

Finally, I'm indebted to my family and special friends. I have the great advantage in my life to be loved by people far better than I, who endure my impatience, show me kindness when I am truly undeserving, and stand by me in troubled times. Friedrich Nietzsche once wrote, "He who has a why to live for can bear with almost any how." These wonderful people are my "why." My heartfelt thanks to all.

Chapter 1

Remembering Ben

Sophie Bloom

Editor's note: This chapter was included as the foreword for the first edition of this book. Sophie Bloom, Ben's beloved wife, passed away in May 2010.

Professor Thomas Guskey, one of my husband's outstanding doctoral students, collected the stories in this book based on the experiences of former students and colleagues of Ben Bloom. Tom worked very hard at editing the book and getting it published. In addition, it was Tom's idea to include the reference inside the back cover giving readers access to Ben's lecture given at Woodward Court on the University of Chicago campus on February 27, 1977. This lecture was part of the "From the Midway" faculty lecture series sponsored by Professor Izaak Wirszup and his wife, Pera. In this lecture, Ben describes his ideas and presents some of his basic research.

Tom also convinced me to write this foreword. In it, I will try to describe the theme that provided the foundation for Ben's research over more than five decades and also include some personal anecdotes about Ben.

Ben was a true pioneer in educational research and, early on, believed that research in education needed to take a more global approach. I was surprised when he first told me of thinking about education in terms of the whole world. I thought, "What a dreamer!" But my world was much smaller than his. The vision he held was decades ahead of our current acceptance of the concept of "global economy." Indeed, Ben became a world guru of education.

Ben was first involved in world education when the Ford Foundation sent him to India in 1957 to conduct a series of workshops on evaluation. Despite the Indian educators' initial suspicion and rejection of the term

1

"workshop," which to them meant "manual labor," Ben won them over. While in Delhi, Ben observed a college student in a park, pacing back and forth, memorizing the contents of a book. Ben knew that this kind of activity was typical of education throughout the world at the time, where 90 percent of learning was at the lowest level of the *Taxonomy*—the "knowledge" level. In the workshops that Ben conducted with educators in several cities in India, he demonstrated that rote knowledge lasted only long enough for students to pass the exam, and very little became permanent. He convinced the Indian educators that students needed to learn the skills associated with higher mental processes. Specifically, they needed to learn how to apply the knowledge they were acquiring and, if they did so, the thinking skills they developed would be lifelong.

Ben was invited back to India the following summer to conduct more workshops. Following his visit, the government of India sent ten educators to the University of Chicago for a year to study with Ben and other faculty members. This led to a complete revision of the examination system in India. It was also the beginning of Ben's work as an educational advisor and consultant to countries around the world.

As university examiner at the University of Chicago, Ben was instrumental in shifting the instructional emphasis from teaching facts to teaching students how to use the knowledge they had learned. With Ben's help, professors in the College found that they were able to help students who were weak problem solvers to develop the skills involved in these higher mental processes. As a result, students were permitted to use their notes and books during comprehensive exams, but were challenged to apply their knowledge in order to solve new problems in diverse situations.

Ben was convinced, backed by significant research evidence, that *what any person can learn, all can learn*, except perhaps for the lowest 1 or 2 percent of students. The task of the school was not to weed out the poor learners and encourage good learners. To quote Ben, "Education must be increasingly concerned about the fullest development of *all* children and youth, and it will be the responsibility of the school to seek learning conditions that enable each individual to reach the highest level of learning possible for her or him" (Bloom, Hastings & Madaus, 1971, p. 6).

Because so many teachers in those early years accepted normal-curve distributions as an acceptable outcome of teaching, they justified large numbers of failures and lots of low achievers. Ben said, "We need large numbers of people with high-level skills who like to learn, and we're not going to get them with an educational system designed to ensure that most students fail. We need to replace this antiquated system with one that produces very few failures" (Bloom, Hastings & Madaus, 1971, p. 6).

Ben was deeply concerned about the negative effect of doing poorly in school or failing on the self-image of children. He wrote, "To be physically (and legally) imprisoned for 10 or 12 years and to receive negative classification repeatedly for this period of time must have a major detrimental effect on personality and character development" (Bloom, Hastings & Madaus, 1971, p. 7). The second volume of the *Taxonomy*, which focused on the affective domain, recognizes that students learn much more in school than academic subjects. Much of what they learn involves interests, values, and social skills. Ben believed that the most important learning that takes place in school may have to do with such feelings—both positive and negative.

Ben's determination to ensure the learning success of all students led to the introduction of his theory on mastery learning. This instructional process used the same teachers and the same material, but added feedback and correctives at regular intervals. When well implemented, approximately 80 percent of the students in mastery learning classes earned As and Bs, compared to only 20 percent in control classes. Under mastery learning, students' rate of learning and motivation to learn also became more similar. In one of his talks at the American Educational Research Association (AERA) Conference, Ben stated that under instructional conditions like those provided by mastery learning, the differences between high and low achievers would reach a "vanishing point"—a comment that stunned many in his audience. Mastery learning became very popular worldwide at all levels of education, from primary to professional levels. Some of the effects of mastery learning include:

- Increased student self-assurance
- Reduced competition and encouraged cooperation among students; that is, students were enabled to help one another
- Assessments became learning tools rather than official grades
- Students were given a second chance at success

One of the conditions necessary for mastery learning was determining the prerequisites needed before instruction. One of Ben's students, Fernando Leyton, explored this in his doctoral dissertation research, teaching students the course prerequisites for second-year algebra and second-year French. After students were helped to learn the course prerequisites, mastery learning was used in teaching the courses. The average mastery learning student scored higher than 95 percent of students in the control class on course final exams. Leyton later applied what his research had taught him to his own daughter's education. She was South American, struggling in her Chicago high school classes, and ready to drop out of school. With his help on prerequisites, she became an excellent student and graduated with honors.

Ben also used mastery learning in his own graduate classes, insisting that all students reach a high learning criterion at regular intervals throughout the course. I remember when our neighbor, who was a student in one of Ben's classes, was so very excited when she earned her A. Ben made it a point to be personally involved with his graduate students and took great interest in their learning. He spent an inordinate amount of time with each.

Ben's life was a life of ideas—big ideas. He had the instinctive ability to examine every facet of a new idea, discard the inessentials, and reveal the core. He also had the ability to project what would be important ten years and more in the future. He tried to instill this in his students, along with his optimism, his sense of humor, and his sense of mission. His students came from all parts of the world to study in the Measurement, Evaluation, and Statistical Analysis (MESA) Program that Ben originated within the Department of Education at the University of Chicago. Many MESA students went on to make significant contributions to education and became leaders in their fields.

Realizing that group instruction produced errors in learning, Ben encouraged two of his doctoral students to do their research on the outcomes of engaging randomly selected students in one-to-one tutoring. The results were spectacular. The tutored students performed as well as the top 2 percent of students in control classes. Realizing that one-to-one tutoring was impractical in most school contexts, however, Ben decided that the next step would be to find teaching and learning methods that could be used in group-based classrooms that would be as effective as one-to-one tutoring. Since the 98th percentile was equivalent to two sigmas (i.e., two standard deviations), Ben labeled this the "2 Sigma Problem."

I attended the session at the AERA Conference when Ben proposed his 2 sigma challenge. Professor Anne Peterson introduced him. She said that most educational researchers were pleased to get an improvement of a fraction of one sigma, or one sigma at most, but not Ben Bloom. He was aiming for a *two sigma* improvement. In his presentation, Ben said that by using a combination of mastery learning and effective parent support, as well as other factors that research data showed could yield significant improvements, that two sigma improvements were both possible and attainable. In the years that followed, many of his students continued to do research on the 2 sigma challenge.

Ben believed that parents were extremely important in the education of their children. He especially emphasized their importance in the Head Start Program, for which he had provided critical supporting research when the program was initiated under President Lyndon Johnson.

Ben also had an insatiable curiosity about the world. He was a voracious reader and a thorough researcher. He read everything and remembered well what he read. As a child in Lansford, Pennsylvania, the librarian would not allow him to return books that he had checked out earlier that same day until he was able to convince her that he had, indeed, read them completely.

While a fellow in the Center for the Advanced Study of the Behavioral Sciences in Palo Alto, California, Ben was freed from department meetings and a hectic teaching schedule. This time allowed him to explore his idea, revolutionary at the time, that much of an individual's development takes place in early childhood. Most of the research in education then emphasized learning at the secondary school and college levels.

Ben spent long hours every day at the center exploring and analyzing research to substantiate his theory. His findings were later published in the book, *Stability and Change in Human Characteristics*, which demonstrated that, indeed, more than half of an individual's cognitive development takes place by four years of age. President Lyndon Johnson invited Ben to come to Washington and testify before Congress about his findings. Based largely on the evidence Ben presented, President Johnson signed the Economic Opportunity Act in 1964, and the Head Start Program was born.

Ben was not particularly good at keeping copies of his work, and I was very upset that I did not have a single copy of *Stability and Change*. So our son, Jonathan, knowing how much I wanted a copy, found one for me through the Internet. What a wonderful gift.

Ben had a passion for his work, and a childlike enthusiasm for describing it. Students, colleagues, and friends all recall how Ben would jump up from his desk, go to his blackboard, draw a normal curve, and then superimpose highly skewed curves to demonstrate possible and achievable learning outcomes.

Professor Susan Stoldosky, one of Ben's first doctoral students who later became a Professor of Education at the University of Chicago, planned a celebration for Ben's retirement from the university. The celebration included a two-day seminar and a large dinner. Several prominent educators spoke at the dinner, including Ralph Tyler, David Krathwohl, and Torsten Husén of Sweden. Ben Wright, one of Ben's faculty colleagues in the MESA Program, was also scheduled to speak. When it came Ben Wright's turn, he wheeled in a large portable blackboard with three curves prominently drawn, describing it as Ben Bloom's personal logo; his personal signature. And it was certainly true. Ben took great joy in greeting all of his current and former students, his colleagues, friends, and relatives at this celebration.

Ben also played a very special role in the lives of his friends. He was the person they turned to when they had a problem, personal or professional. At many times it seemed he was everyone's unofficial advisor.

First it was friends and students, and then it became the friends' and students' children, and then the children themselves. Then came nieces and nephews and their spouses. And, of course, he was always available for our sons and for me.

Ben was co-founder of the International Association for the Evaluation of Educational Achievement (IEA). It began as a group of educators from twelve countries who met in Hamburg, Germany. From the very beginning, the group was concerned about financial backing. A German corporation had promised assistance but then backed out. One night while in Hamburg, Ben received a telegram from a U.S. government official stating that his request for assistance had been approved and the required funds would be provided. Ben immediately telephoned all of his colleagues and asked them to come down to the lobby and to bring their toothbrush glasses. Somewhat grudgingly, they all trooped down in their nightclothes, glasses in hand. After making his announcement that funding had been secured, Ben proposed a toast in French Armagnac. The IEA was officially born.

Much to the amazement of the world, the United States did not lead in the first IEA assessment in the field of mathematics. Japanese students scored the highest. The next step was to analyze the Japanese teaching methods to determine how they attained these outstanding results. Through this effort in international cooperation, the countries learned from one another. As time went on, many more countries joined the IEA effort. Torsten Husén was appointed the first president and Neville Postlethwaite was appointed the first executive director. IEA was initially located in the UNESCO Institute for Education in Hamburg, Germany, from 1960 to 1969, when it was moved to Sweden at the request of Torsten Husén. In the early 1980s it was moved to the Netherlands.

In 1971, Ben convinced his IEA colleagues to sponsor the International Seminar for Advanced Training in Curriculum Development and Innovation, which was held in Gränna, Sweden. Ben and Neville Postlethwaite planned the seminar, and Ben served as the seminar director. By that time the IEA had grown to include twenty-nine countries worldwide, including Poland, which was then part of the Soviet Union.

The seminar used a team approach, based on the premise that each team would go back to their native country and establish their own curriculum research center to expand and refine the work. Each team consisted of specialists in six fields:

1. Administration
2. Educational evaluation
3. Science education
4. Social studies education

5. Elementary education
6. Humanities (literature and language)

Every team met each morning for a lecture or presentation by an international expert in curriculum or instruction. In the afternoon, members met separately for subject-specific discussions led by an expert in their respective fields. Ralph Tyler gave many of the morning lectures and served as general consultant to all.

It was thrilling to watch the opening ceremony with team members wearing their native dress. The members of the team from the Netherlands had borrowed outfits from a museum in Amsterdam to wear that day. How colorful were the native clothes worn by the Nigerians, the Ghanaians, the Hindu Indians, the Argentineans, the Koreans, the Japanese, and the other twenty-two national teams. Morale could not have been higher. Each team was eager to learn how to improve the way children learned in their countries. As a result of the Gränna seminar, many teams developed and improved their curriculum research centers in their native countries. Ben visited each center during the following year to support and advise them on their work.

The next seminar sponsored by IEA met in Legon, Ghana, near Accra, in 1974. This was a six-week seminar that included teams from fifteen English-speaking African countries. Again, the presenters were international and highly diverse. The seminar was carefully planned by Ben, Neville, and Endre Bailer of Hungary. It was the first time these countries had met to discuss and share the educational concerns of the continent of Africa. Ralph Tyler was in charge for the first three weeks and Ben for the last three weeks. To my surprise, Ben asked me to give one of the lectures. I spoke to the group about applying "principles of learning" to help students be successful. I had used these ideas with great success in training teachers in the Chicago Public Schools, and they were very well received by the African educators.

In 1986, Ben served as an exchange scholar to China. He was one of twenty-five educators selected to be among the first exchange scholars between the United States and China. Three of the exchange scholars were Distinguished Service Professors from the University of Chicago. They included Professor Clyde Hutchison in chemistry, Professor Hu in history, and Ben in education. Ben had been selected by Dr. Lin Fu Nian, Honorary President of the prestigious Shanghai Normal University. Of course, the Chinese are not known to be particularly demonstrative with strangers, and Ben was no different. But much to my amazement, when Ben and Dr. Nian met for the first time, they warmly embraced each other.

In China, Ben and I were treated like royalty. Dr. Lin Fu Nian organized a seminar of five hundred outstanding Chinese educators from all parts of China to convene in Shanghai for a week of study and discussion with Ben. The seminar began with an impressive ceremony, attended by the mayor of Shanghai, to introduce Ben formally and to bestow upon him an honorary professorship. Fortunately for us, everything was translated into English. Then, as is the custom in China, two lovely children came to the platform and presented each of us with beautiful bouquets of flowers.

Ben also presented lectures in several cities in different parts of China. Prior to our arrival, Dr. Lin Fu Nian had arranged to have a million copies of Bloom's *Taxonomy* translated into Chinese and distributed to educators throughout the country. It was quite an experience! Years later, a young Chinese American woman approached me at an AERA conference and said, "You know, Mrs. Bloom, they are studying 'Bloom' all over China."

Ben was especially devoted to his family and his nieces and nephews. He had been a handball champion in college, and taught our sons both handball and Ping-Pong. Janet, our niece, described at Ben's funeral her fond experiences with Uncle Ben in our basement, saying, "Picture Ben, racing from side to side with the agility of a tournament table tennis player as he womped us with his Chinese backhand."

Ben also taught our sons to play chess, and they were among twelve simultaneous contenders against Adrian DeGroot, an international chess champion from the Netherlands, during our time at the Center in California. Of course, DeGroot won all twelve games, including one in which the board was hidden from him behind a large blackboard. Ben also made our sons beautiful slingshots one time when we were camping, though I sometimes doubted the wisdom of that. He built a roller coaster in our basement that provided hours of entertainment. One summer he taught six neighborhood boys how to type and compose stories on their own typewriters. They came to our home early each morning with their portable typewriters and for an hour typed away.

Ben was also quite an inventor. Together with our son David, he made an impact-absorbing rubber bumper for automobiles. The two of them did research to obtain the best quality rubber that would endure crashes. They then attached the bumpers to cars and conducted tests by crashing into old, abandoned wrecks. After several failed trials, they came upon a design that worked, much to their amazement. We ended up with lots of boxes of rubber bumpers in our basement. Obviously, Ben and David were much better inventors than they were salesmen.

The two of them also developed a plastic, erasable, translator card for travelers. The card used common words in English, Spanish, and French. David, at age seventeen, was appointed to approach the vice president of Braniff Airlines in Texas to order a large quantity. It was nearly successful, but once again the Bloom family ended up with numerous boxes of translators in our basement.

Ben was always ready to help anyone in need. One night we heard screams coming from outside. Ben immediately ran out of the house, ignoring his own safety and not even stopping to grab a coat, to see if he could help. Just down the street he found a woman who had been mugged and had her purse stolen. Ben invited her back to our home, offered her some tea, and did his best to calm and comfort her.

During his career in education, Ben won many awards and honorary degrees. He was elected president of the American Educational Research Association and held high-level offices in many professional organizations. He was also one of the cofounders of the International Academy of Education in Belgium. In June 1998, under the leadership of several of his former students in India, the Benjamin Bloom International Academy of Education was dedicated near Delhi. It was a wonderful tribute for which Ben felt tremendously honored. In truth, Ben was an exceptionally modest man about everything but his title—the Charles Swift Distinguished Service Professor. This endowed professorship was previously held by Enrico Fermi, and Ben felt uniquely honored to have it.

Through the efforts of Professor David Krathwohl, Ben's first research assistant at the University of Chicago and coauthor of the *Taxonomy*; John Craig, acting dean of education; and Noel Salinger, vice president for development and alumni affairs at the University of Chicago; we were able to establish the Benjamin Bloom Dissertation Fellowship. The first two exceptionally talented recipients completed their dissertations in the field of education at the University of Chicago. The third recipient will be selected for the coming year.

Ben helped me write my master's degree thesis and urged me to complete my book on peer tutoring in the schools. I wish to thank Tom Guskey for similarly convincing me to write this foreword about Ben. It has turned out to be a special, unexpected gift to me, in spite of my original reluctance to write it.

A proper end to this forward is Ben's quote about the central purpose of his research: "These are operations to enable teachers to realize the seductive dream which drew them into education—the fullest development of the students" (Bloom, Hastings & Madaus, 1971, p. vii).

Chapter 2

Unlimited Expectations

Thomas R. Guskey

In 1981 I left my position then as assistant professor of education at the University of Kentucky to become the first director of research at the Center for the Improvement of Teaching and Learning, a national educational research center established in Chicago. The center's charge was to find exceptionally effective but cost-efficient ways to alter instructional conditions so that more students achieved at high levels and gained the many positive benefits of learning success. One of my first tasks as director was to appoint a board of advisors and, naturally, I called upon my former advisor and dissertation committee chair, Ben Bloom, who graciously accepted my invitation.

Together we outlined an extremely ambitious research agenda for the center. Our plan was to conduct an extensive series of small-scale pilot studies testing the viability of several low-cost ways to improve student learning, especially at the post-secondary level. Once we determined the effectiveness of these different strategies, we hoped to bring together the leaders of the major community college systems throughout the nation, share our findings with them, and enlist their cooperation in continuing the work with larger, more extensive studies.

That first year proved a difficult and grueling experience. The studies became more complicated than we expected and unanticipated political problems consistently arose to thwart our efforts. Fourteen-hour days were not uncommon and weekends became indistinguishable from weekdays. But in the end, the long hours and dedicated effort paid off. Our studies were remarkably successful and most of the major community college systems from across the country agreed to send delegates to a conference we organized in Chicago to discuss the work and to extend these initial efforts.

On the morning the conference was to begin, Ben met me at the center, and we walked together to the hotel in downtown Chicago where the conference was being held. Our conversation along the way reflected on the many challenges that had been encountered but also the excitement that both of us felt about what had been accomplished. At one point along the way, however, he turned to me and said, "You know, Tom, I never thought this would be possible."

His comment stunned me completely and I stopped, mid-stride, glaring at him in disbelief. "What do you mean, you never thought this would be possible?" I asked, not bothering to conceal my astonishment and accompanying anger. "You told me from the start that this is what you expected. I worked myself to a frazzle this year making sure it happened. And now you tell me you never thought it would be possible! How could you do that to me?"

Sensing my anger, Ben stopped and turned to me smiling. "Tom," he said, "I've never let my expectations be limited by what I thought was possible. You need to do the same. . . ."

As we turned and walked on I realized that in that simple, eloquent statement, he revealed to me the premise that guided his life's work. Our vision of what we can and should expect need not be limited by what we believe to be possible. Rather, it is by expecting the impossible that we attain our greatest achievements.

Chapter 3

"Typically We Will Find . . ."

Lawrence Hecht

In graduate courses where students learn about research methods and techniques, their professors always stress the importance of formulating hypotheses—educated guesses about expected results. Hypotheses provide focus and direction in investigations. They establish the basis for selecting research methods and designs, as well as for choosing the procedures used to analyze relevant data.

Unfortunately, researchers today too often proceed without clearly formulated hypotheses. They charge headlong into investigations under the banner of "exploration," having little idea of what they are looking for, what they hope to find, or what the possible implications of their findings might be.

Ben was never that way. He approached research problems very systematically and insisted that his students do the same. Early in their studies at the University of Chicago, for instance, he insisted that all students read John Platt's article on "strong inference" (Platt, 1964) and apply the process Platt outlined for developing primary and alternative hypotheses to a problem that was of interest to them. When it came time to work on their dissertations, he often recommended they return to the Platt article and renew their understanding of the process.

In his own research, Ben did the same. With careful thought and deliberation he would develop his theory. Next he formulated his hypotheses based on that theory, along with possible alternatives. Finally he searched for evidence either to confirm or to refute his hypotheses. Of course, because of his careful preparation and forethought, he was always confident of confirmation rather than refutation.

Lawrence Hecht, a former student of Ben's who served as a senior research scientist with the College Board, saw this as one of Ben's finest qualities as a researcher. Noting the systematic nature of Ben's thinking and the confidence it gave him led Larry to make the following rather humorous observation. He described Ben as "the only person I've ever known who uses the word 'typically' in the future tense—as in his often-used phrase, 'Typically we will find.'"

Indeed, because of his insightful reflection, perceptive reasoning, and thorough preparation, Ben knew what he was looking for and was confident of the results before he ever began his research. And his confidence was infectious. Occasionally his hypotheses were proven false, of course, but very rarely.

Chapter 4

It's More Than Numbers

Elliot W. Eisner

One of Ben's most remarkable talents was his ability to view educational problems and issues from a variety of different perspectives. This allowed him to gain insights that eluded most others. It also allowed him to see beyond narrow quantitative interpretations of research findings and to discover unnoticed but extremely important theoretical or practical implications. Elliot Eisner, professor emeritus of education and art at Stanford University and former student of Ben's, saw an example of this during one of his classes with Ben at the University of Chicago:

"I was a member of a graduate class of Ben's in which students were asked to present proposals for their dissertations or to describe pilot studies they had completed in preparation for their dissertation research. After several weeks of presentations it finally came my turn to present. The dissertation I planned focused on the measurement of different types of creativity displayed in two- and three-dimensional artwork made by children who were ten and eleven years of age. The criteria I had conceptualized for identifying each of the four types of creativity were complex and not immediately obvious. The tasks the judges confronted required them to make assessments based on subtle but important aspects of the creative features of the students' artwork.

"Despite my best efforts, the interrater reliability correlation coefficients turned out to be only .40 to .50—a point of some embarrassment to me. Writing these coefficients on the board drew snickers from several of my classmates, many of whom were majoring in quantitative research methods. Ben, sitting in the back of the room, was visibly irritated by the response. He immediately rose from his seat, went directly to the board and, much to my surprise, showed how significant such coefficients were in light of the complexity of the tasks the judges were asked to perform.

"Ben's demonstration made a lasting impression on all class members and especially me. I recall two lessons from that day that were particularly poignant. The first is the importance of supporting students in difficult times. Ben believed that nothing positive was ever gained by embarrassing a student. Embarrassment, he insisted, was a poor motivator and a worse teacher. The second lesson is the value of always putting statistics in context. How one interprets a set of numbers depends not only on matters of measurement but also on the characteristics of the situation from which those numbers are derived. Both are lessons that I never forgot.

"Ben's commitment to the possibilities of education provided a unique kind of inspiration to all those who studied with him. He was an optimist, but an optimist who looked to the facts and who designed studies to give substance to his aspirations."

Chapter 5

The Early Years

Thomas R. Guskey

Benjamin Samuel Bloom was born in Lansford, Pennsylvania, a small town in the northeastern part of the state, on February 21, 1913. His parents were Russian immigrants who came to the United States in hopes of building a better life for their family and to escape growing persecution of the Jews in Russia. His father worked as a picture framer and his mother was a housewife who loved flower gardening. He had three older brothers and a younger sister.

Ben attended public grammar school and public high school in rural Lansford, excelling both academically and athletically, particularly in the sports of swimming and handball. From his earliest years he was an avid reader and often frustrated the school librarian by attempting to return books on the same day he checked them out. Convinced that no one of his age could read a book so quickly, the librarian refused to accept his books until he had kept them for at least one day.

He graduated from high school in 1931 as the class valedictorian and enrolled at Pennsylvania State University on an academic scholarship. Although he worked several jobs to support himself while in school, Ben completed both his bachelor's and master's degrees in psychology in four years. He also continued his athletic pursuits and, during his senior year, won the university's intramural handball championship.

Following his graduation, Ben worked briefly at a state prison outside of Harrisburg, Pennsylvania, and then took a job as a research worker with the Pennsylvania State Relief Organization. After one year he moved to Washington, DC, where he took a similar position with the American Youth Commission.

During his second year with the commission, Ben attended a meeting at which Ralph W. Tyler spoke. At the time Tyler had already gained some renown as a psychometrician and was involved in designing assessments for his classic Eight-Year Study of Progressive Education (Aikin, 1942; Smith & Tyler, 1942). Tyler's presentation thoroughly impressed the young psychologist from Pennsylvania. With his photographic memory, Tyler was able to recall the minutest details of others' work and offered insights that were amazingly clear and poignant.

Shortly thereafter Tyler was invited to serve as a reviewer of reports issued by the American Youth Commission, many of which Ben helped to prepare. As much as he looked forward to these opportunities to work with Tyler, the process also proved exceptionally frustrating for Ben. After spending months working on a report and being convinced that he had derived everything possible from the data collected, Tyler would glance through the report for a few minutes and find aspects and nuances that Ben had missed. Yet despite his frustration with Tyler, when Ben decided to continue his graduate education, he knew that he wanted to study with Tyler.

So after three years with the commission, Ben applied and was accepted in the doctoral program at Ohio State University where Tyler was on the faculty. After submitting his application, however, Ben found out that Tyler had left Ohio State and had taken a position at the University of Chicago, Tyler's alma mater. Despite misgivings about attending a "city college," Ben immediately withdrew his application to Ohio State and applied to the doctoral program at Chicago. He was admitted and began his doctoral studies under Tyler's direction in the summer of 1939.

During his first year at Chicago, Ben met the love of his life, Sophie, in the education library on the University of Chicago campus. She was working on her master's degree at the university at the time. Ben was immediately smitten and proposed marriage one week after their first meeting. They didn't become formally engaged until the following spring, however, and were married in the summer of 1940 in Detroit, Michigan.

Ben and Sophie made their home in Hyde Park, near the University of Chicago campus, and became active in many community affairs. Together they raised two sons: Jonathan, a tax accountant in Chicago, and David, a professional musician who founded and directs the Bloom School of Jazz, also in Chicago. Their home was a warm and friendly place where Ben and Sophie frequently entertained and family members often gathered. Nieces and nephews still tell stories of the fun they had while visiting the Blooms' home and of fierce table tennis games in the basement with "Uncle Ben."

Ben's commitment to social justice was evident even in those early years. One winter evening during dinner the Bloom family heard a commotion outside their house. A woman's purse had been stolen and she was calling for help. Without an instant of hesitation, Ben raced out of the house, forgetting even a coat, and ran down the street to offer aid. When someone needed help, he was never one to stand idly by and ignore the call. More often he was the first to offer his assistance.

Chapter 6
Strength in Simplicity

James H. Block

In the early 1960s, Ben was primarily responsible for founding the University of Chicago Department of Education's doctoral program in Measurement, Evaluation, and Statistical Analysis (MESA), the premier quantitative methodology training program of its time in educational research. Despite his extensive knowledge of quantitative methods, however, Ben was widely perceived by students as being perhaps the least quantitatively sophisticated of the MESA faculty members. In his own research he typically used uncomplicated methods such as simple and partial correlations, and regression analyses. Still, time after time at doctoral dissertation defenses that frequently dealt with newly developed and highly sophisticated quantitative techniques, Ben more than held his own, regularly asking the most thoughtful and probing questions.

James Block, retired professor of education at the University of California at Santa Barbara and former student of Ben's, made note of this in the following story:

"I once asked Ben how he had developed such insight into the power of simpler rather than more complex statistical techniques for the analysis of educational data. He told me that he'd learned the power of simple techniques during his days as a doctoral student at the University of Chicago, working under the direction of Ralph Tyler. His dissertation research required him to calculate innumerable simple and partial correlations by hand, without the aid of modern calculators or computers.

"It made sense to me that calculating so many correlations by hand might have been instructive, but it still didn't explain the special insight Ben seemed to have about the ins and outs of correlations as a powerful data analysis technique. After some probing, he finally confessed to me that what I perceived as 'insight' had not come from doing all the calculations himself, but from having his wife Sophie's help.

"On one particular occasion shortly after they were married, Ben convinced Sophie to help him calculate a large number of time-consuming, complex correlations. Only after all the calculations were completed did Ben discover that he'd given Sophie a wrong and overly complex formula for the calculations. Needless to say, the stress in the young Blooms' marriage was considerable for a brief period. It was during that time, however, that Ben vowed to learn inside and out the statistical technique that he had mistaken. He also vowed to never inflict upon others what he had inflicted on his wife, namely, the use of more complicated techniques when simpler and more elegant ones would do."

Chapter 7

The Best in the World

Thomas R. Guskey

Although he received numerous, highly lucrative offers from other institutions, Ben spent his entire professional career at the University of Chicago. He served briefly on the faculty at Northwestern University after retiring from his position at Chicago, but more as a favor to his friend and former colleague, David Wiley, who was then dean of the School of Education at Northwestern.

Ben's stature in the field of education and the eminence of his work added greatly to the prominence of the University of Chicago. He strongly believed, however, that the university's support had been instrumental to his success. The University of Chicago epitomized to Ben what a truly great university should be: a place where the pursuit of knowledge and high academic ideals took precedence over all else. As a result, his loyalty and devotion to the University of Chicago was unquestionable. He also made no secret of the honor he felt in being a faculty member there and the esteem in which he held its hallowed halls.

I came to understand Ben's feelings about the University of Chicago in a particularly memorable way. While completing my master's degree program at Boston College, I was persuaded by Professor John Walsh to consider continuing my studies at the University of Chicago in the Measurement, Evaluation, and Statistical Analysis (MESA) Program headed by Ben. Professor Walsh had received his doctorate at the University of Chicago in quantitative inquiry under the direction of Ralph Tyler, and had developed a friendship with Ben during that time. As chair of the educational research department at Boston College, Professor Walsh had modeled their program after the University of Chicago's program. He still believed, however, that Chicago's MESA Program was clearly the preeminent program.

With Professor Walsh's help, along with that of other Boston College faculty members who were also University of Chicago alumni or friends of Ben's, namely Peter Airasian and George Madaus, I applied and was accepted in the MESA Program. But being young, stubborn, and unwilling to take unquestioned the advice of others, I also applied to several other prestigious programs, gaining acceptance to them as well. So in the spring of 1975, I set out from Boston to visit the various campuses and to meet some of the people with whom I might be studying. Chicago was the last stop on my trip.

From the moment my plane touched down at O'Hare Airport in Chicago, I felt a sense of gloom. The weather in Chicago on that particular day was downright nasty—snowing, sometimes sleeting, and always windy. The damp, icy cold cut through me like a sharp knife, defying all my efforts to keep warm. I had grown accustomed to cold weather in Boston, of course, but this was a different kind of cold—bitterer and meaner.

The cab ride from the airport to the university campus lasted over an hour and took me past mostly factories and rows of tenements. What I remember most about the trip, however, was the ubiquitous gray. The sky, the lake, the streets, the buildings, and even the people—everything was gray. I sat in the backseat of the cab watching the meter click away to an amount far greater than I had budgeted and thinking mostly about what other means of transportation I could find back to the airport.

As we finally approached the university campus my sense of gloom grew worse. The Gothic architecture of the university buildings seemed a perfect match to the cold and miserable weather. Gargoyles peered down from the rooftops of the campus buildings adding a grotesque element to the dreariness. Faceless people, some in rain ponchos and others with wind-torn umbrellas, scurried about in frantic efforts to find shelter from the weather. I sensed that I had wandered into a scene from an Alfred Hitchcock movie.

After a quick campus tour I was scheduled to meet Ben in his office in Judd Hall, named for Charles Hubbard Judd, the eminent educational psychologist who sought to develop a science of education. Cold, wet, and now with a sullen disposition, I approached his open office door at the end of a long hallway. Inside sat the most pleasant looking man, reclining in his office chair, feet propped up on his desk, reading a book. "Mr. Guskey?" he asked on noticing me. I nodded. "Fine," he replied, "I've been waiting to meet you." And he rose from his chair, extending his hand to greet me.

He was not at all what I expected. My Boston College professors spoke of Benjamin Bloom with such reverence and esteem that I imagined him to be a giant. The man coming toward me was five feet seven at best. He had a stocky but athletic build with short, silvery hair brushed straight back. He shook my hand firmly and invited me to take a chair beside his desk.

Entering his office on the left was a large table piled high with papers and books that appeared to be in no particular order. Beside the table was a small, wheeled stand that held a blue, IBM Selectric typewriter. On the right side of the office stood a series of bookshelves. Most prominent was a shelf in the center that held a large collection of maroon-colored University of Chicago doctoral dissertations. As I walked by I noticed many familiar names: Richard Wolf, Peter Airasian, Edward Kifer, James Block, Lorin Anderson, . . . These were some of the people whose work I had been reading in my classes at Boston College.

Opposite his desk chair was a chalkboard on which two different frequency distributions were neatly drawn. One appeared to be a normal, bell-shaped curve while the other was highly skewed with most of the observations clustered on the right side of the distribution. Soon I would learn that this was the basis of his work on mastery learning.

Beside the chalkboard hung a photograph of a distinguished-looking, bald gentleman with dark framed glasses. As I took off my damp coat and sat down, I asked if that was a photograph of his father. "Sort of," Ben replied. "That's Ralph Tyler. He was the chair of my doctoral committee when I was a student here at Chicago." I later learned that the photograph of Tyler was one of the few portraits done by famed photographer Ansel Adams.

Our conversation, like his office, was warm and friendly, and soon my gloominess began to fade. He asked about my work at Boston College and his friends and former students on the faculty there. We talked about the MESA Program at the University of Chicago and all that it offered. And knowing that I was considering programs at other institutions, we also talked about those.

"What you must consider, Mr. Guskey," Ben began, "are the people at those institutions who are doing really important, cutting-edge work in the field of education. Larger research universities may have eighty to a hundred faculty members in their schools of education. But among those, perhaps twelve or fifteen are doing that kind of important, cutting-edge work. Here at Chicago, we have only thirty-five faculty members in our Department of Education. But we have thirty-five of those kinds of people."

"So then, Professor Bloom," I asked, "would you consider this to be the best program in the country in this area?"

At first he appeared surprised by my question, as if the answer should have been obvious. He leaned forward in his chair, looked me straight in the eye with great seriousness, and replied, ". . . in the *world!*"

Thomas R. Guskey

His answer left no doubt about what he believed. It was also obvious that to him, this was not a matter of opinion—it was fact. In this area, the University of Chicago was without equal. Those with whom I had met at other institutions spoke highly of their programs, but no one was as clear, as unequivocal, or as convincing.

We continued to talk about other aspects of the program, the department, and the university. But at that point my decision was made. Six months later I began my doctoral studies in the MESA Program at the University of Chicago, with Ben as my advisor and eventual chair of my dissertation committee.

Copyright © Marc PoKempner. Used with permission.

Copyright © Marc PoKempner. Used with permission.

Copyright © Marc PoKempner. Used with permission.

Chapter 8

Using Time Wisely

George Engelhard, Jr.

Because of his many involvements, Ben's schedule was always filled. His university commitments, his worldwide travels, and his regular writing took up the major portion of his professional time. But even during his most hectic periods of work, he always reserved time for his students.

To make certain that he shared his time equitably among his students, however, Ben established a unique "sign-up" system. Every Monday morning he posted a sign-up sheet outside of his office in Judd Hall, listing his office hours on Tuesday divided into fifteen-minute intervals. Students lined up to select their fifteen minutes of Ben's undivided attention. Occasionally the time was spent discussing coursework or different aspects of the Measurement, Evaluation, or Statistical Analysis (MESA) Program. But more often discussions focused on some facet of the students' dissertation research.

In addition to these voluntary meetings, Ben also used this time to ensure students' steady progress in completing their degrees. He pressed students relentlessly to finish their coursework, write their dissertations, and then go on to make important professional contributions. He recognized that students invest a great deal in the University of Chicago in order to gain their degree. But the university likewise invested in them—an investment that to Ben carried significant responsibility. It obliged students to add to the field of education by conducting research, by teaching, or by helping to shape educational policy.

To guarantee that students not neglect their work, Ben often "insisted" that they sign up for a fifteen-minute time slot each week. He referred to these meetings as "required opportunities" and used them to keep students focused on making progress. George Engelhard, Jr., professor of education at Emory University and former student of Ben's, remembers these meetings in this way:

"To me, these weekly meetings with Ben were similar to the weekly music lessons I experienced as a child: attendance was required, whether you were ready or not. Like a strict music teacher, Ben was more than a little annoyed if you were not properly prepared and expressed his hope that you would not disappoint him again. When that happened, the meeting usually ended quickly, but always provided the necessary incentive to make sure that you never repeated the same offense. When you were prepared, however, Ben's approval was obvious. And the personal guidance and direction he offered at those times always proved invaluable to me, as I'm sure it did to many others."

And did these "required opportunities" work? The record speaks for itself. Not only did nearly every one of Ben's students graduate, but over two-thirds became professors at major universities, many growing to be renowned scholars in their own right. Others went on to serve in leadership positions in prestigious research organizations and educational agencies in the United States and abroad. His legacy was not only profound, it was also broad and long lived.

Chapter 9

The University of Chicago's Board of Examinations

Thomas R. Guskey

Ben's first professional position at the University of Chicago was as a research assistant in the office of the university's Board of Examinations under the direction of Ralph W. Tyler. In addition to his duties as a faculty member in the Department of Education, Tyler also served at that time as the university examiner. Knowing Ben's background in psychometrics, Tyler thought that Ben would be an excellent addition to the board's staff and could help guide the many reforms planned in the university examination process. Ben's affiliation with the Board of Examinations greatly influenced his earliest research at the university and the interests he developed in his later professional career.

The Board of Examinations was founded at the University of Chicago in 1931 and was initially directed by renowned psychologist L. L. Thurstone. In a chapter that Ben wrote for a book edited by Paul Dressel in 1954, he explained the rationale for establishing the board.

> In planning the new curriculum in general education, the faculty wished to separate the examining and judging functions from the pedagogical functions. They wished to have the instructor serve primarily to help students learn, and they believed that an ideal student-teacher relationship was impossible when the teacher also had the responsibility for judging and grading the student. (Bloom, 1954/1981, p. 245)

Ben also noted that University of Chicago faculty wanted to place greater responsibility on students for their own education. Class attendance requirements were dropped and degree requirements in many programs were set exclusively in terms of students' performance on a series of comprehensive examinations. The Board of Examinations was responsible for the quality of these examinations, as well as for their administration and scoring.

Under Thurstone's direction, the board staff focused primarily on developing a technology of testing. Because the examinations usually covered an entire year's worth of instructional content, they tended to be lengthy both in terms of the number of questions and the amount of time students required to complete them. Many of the examinations, for example, included four hundred to six hundred items and required more than six hours to complete (Bloom, 1954/1981). Furthermore, because most of the examinations focused on students' recall of factual information, they were composed mainly of "objective" types of items, such as true/false, matching, and multiple choice. As a result, the board staff concentrated on issues of test construction and administration, scoring procedures, objectivity, reliability, and validity, in both theoretical and practical terms (Richardson, Russell, Snalnaker & Thurstone, 1933; Snalnaker, 1934; Thurstone, 1937; Richardson & Kuder, 1939).

In the latter 1930s, however, the University of Chicago faculty began to question whether students' subject matter knowledge should be the primary goal of instruction. Many believed instead that instruction should help students develop the ability to think, reason, and apply what they know in practical situations. Successful students should be able to address and solve a variety of problems in specific academic disciplines. The fundamental task of general education, therefore, was not simply broadening students' accumulated knowledge, but rather "enabling individuals to understand the world in which they live and to attack the significant problems they encounter both as individuals and as citizens" (Bloom, 1981a, p. 251).

As the faculty increasingly accepted these newly defined learning goals, they began to teach in new and different ways. Quite naturally, this led them to demand different types of examinations that would help them determine how successful they were in helping students to achieve these new learning goals. It also led them to view differently the whole examination process. As Ben described, "Examining had to be seen as part of the total educational process and as having consequences beyond the accurate certification of achievement or beyond the production of good examinations" (Bloom, 1981a, p. 251). It was at this same time, in 1940, that Ralph Tyler succeeded Thurstone as university examiner and brought in Ben to work as a research assistant in the office of the Board of Examinations.

Ben completed his PhD two years later, in the spring of 1942, and received offers from several prestigious universities to join their faculty. But Tyler convinced him to stay on at the University of Chicago and to continue his research in the office of the Board of Examinations. Ben was appointed as an instructor in the university's Department of Education two years later and began his climb through the academic ranks. He remained with the Board of Examinations for two decades, however, from 1940 through 1959, eventually succeeding Tyler as university examiner in 1953.

Most of Ben's writings in the early years of his tenure with the board focused on the relationships among educational goals, methods of instruction, and educational measurement (e.g., Bloom, 1944, 1947b; Bloom & Allison, 1949, 1950). Today these issues are referred to as "instructional alignment," and relate to the association between established standards for student learning, the instructional activities in which teachers engage students, and the procedures used to assess or evaluate student learning. In the late 1940s and early 1950s, Ben began to explore alternative ways of measuring problem solving (Bloom & Broder, 1950) and different approaches to problem solving that resulted from different methods of instruction (Bloom, 1953c, 1954b). At this same time he also began to recognize the need to bring some sense of order to the broad range of cognitive skills tapped by various types of questions and assessment formats. This provided the seeds for developing the *Taxonomy of Educational Objectives, Handbook 1: The Cognitive Domain* (Bloom, 1949; Bloom, Engelhart, Furst, Hill & Krathwohl, 1956; Krathwohl, 1994).

Chapter 10

In the Shadow of Greatness

Thomas R. Guskey

Because of Ben's well-known reputation as an educational leader who consistently produced works of significance, great things also were expected of those who worked with him, especially his students. To be known as a "Bloom student" carried a certain amount of prestige, of course, but it was also a burden of responsibility. This burden not only compelled his students to do good work, it sometimes made it difficult for them to establish their own unique, professional identities. Several of Ben's students struggled mightily to carve out their own special areas of expertise and to develop their own distinct reputations in the field of education.

At the 1982 annual meeting of the American Educational Research Association in New York City, Ben and I, along with Lorin Anderson, a professor of education at the University of South Carolina and also a former student of Ben's, were discussing this issue over dinner one evening. Lorin initiated the discussion by sharing how difficult he had found it to be always introduced as "a student of Benjamin Bloom." Although such an introduction typically drew "ahs" from many in the audience and usually meant that they listened more intently, what they listened for were things they hoped were coming from Ben. To be recognized for the value of your own ideas or your unique contribution seemed rare. Being a more recent graduate, I had not experienced this to the same extent as Lorin, but I nodded in agreement.

Upon hearing Lorin's comment, Ben interrupted his meal, looked at both of us with great seriousness, and shared with us the following bit of advice. "What both of you must remember is this," he began. "When you are my age, I will be dead. But here I am today, nearly seventy, and Ralph Tyler is still alive and very active in education!"

Until that moment I never realized that despite his many accomplishments and the acclaim he had gained among educators throughout the world, Ben still felt that he lived in the shadow of his mentor, Ralph Tyler. To both Lorin and me, Ben's contributions were so great and had far surpassed Tyler's accomplishments, significant as they were. But that is not the way that Ben saw things. The honesty in this admission humbled Lorin and me even more. It also helped us understand more clearly how working with a true giant our field can be both a lifelong advantage as well as a heavy burden to bear.

Chapter 11

Making Expectations Clear

Jeremy Finn and Thomas R. Guskey

Ben made no secret of what he expected from his students, both during their time at the University of Chicago and afterward. I recall one day, during my first year of study in the Measurement, Evaluation, and Statistical Analysis (MESA) Program, I asked Ben about what kinds of professional positions might be available to me should I successfully complete the program. His answer was simple, direct, and unqualified.

"To study here at the University of Chicago," he said, "requires a significant investment of your time and money. But the university, especially this department and its faculty, make an even more important investment in you. We expect that you will go from here and do great things: develop new ideas and understandings, contribute to our field, and teach others. While there are many ways that you might do this, the best is to become a professor at a university where you can develop your own research program and teach promising students."

It was obvious to me that I was not the first student with whom Ben had shared this bit of advice, nor would I be the last. It was also clear that Ben saw this more as an obligation than simply an expectation. To him, it was academic *noblesse oblige* in its purest form. To whom much had been given, much was expected.

Jeremy Finn, professor of education at the State University of New York at Buffalo and a former student of Ben's, shared a similar experience with Ben. Here is his story:

"On the day that I left Chicago to begin my new position as an assistant professor at the State University of New York at Buffalo, I stopped at Judd Hall to say goodbye to several friends and faculty members. While my wife and children waited in our heavily loaded car with a U-Haul trailer attached, I ran from office to office, saying my farewells and receiving many good wishes. Ben was the last person that I visited and, after a short conversation, we walked together back to the waiting car. After saying goodbye to my family, Ben pulled me aside. 'Remember, Jeremy,' he said, 'I expect my students to go out and do the most significant research of all. Don't let me down.'

"Even at that point, Ben was still pushing me. He lived his professional life by a clear set of principles and made them well known to all his students: 'Think carefully about what you are doing, evaluate its significance regularly and thoroughly, and always focus on issues of importance.' He lived up to these principles remarkably well, and forever challenged his students to do likewise."

Chapter 12

Problem-Solving Processes of College Students

Thomas R. Guskey

When Ben began his work in the office of the Board of Examinations, behaviorism was the dominant theory in psychology and education. Ben certainly recognized the powerful implications of behaviorism and its usefulness in many teaching and learning situations. But he was also keenly aware of its inherent limitations. He described these in the introduction to his earliest book, *Problem-Solving Processes of College Students* (Bloom & Broder, 1950):

> Mental processes represent a very difficult and complex subject to study. To a large extent, we have been limited in this study by the widespread emphasis on overt behavior as the major acceptable type of evidence on the workings of the mind. This attempt to make an objective science of psychology not only limits the kinds of data acceptable to psychologists but must necessarily make for many inaccuracies in their inferences about the nature of the mental processes. (p. 1)

This was an amazingly bold statement for a young psychologist to make at that time, especially considering behavioral psychologist L. L. Thurstone's influence at the University of Chicago. Furthermore, Ben made this statement six years before the "mythical birthday of the cognitive revolution" (Bruner, 1992, p. 780).

Problem-Solving Processes of College Students describes the results of three studies conducted at the University of Chicago and coordinated by the Board of Examinations between 1945 and 1948. The problems that formed the basis of these studies were limited to "questions and test situations taken from various academic tests and examinations" (Bloom & Broder, 1950, p. 8). Despite these limitations, however, the researchers empha-

34

sized that they "attempted to select problems for which the subject would have clear-cut, although perhaps quite complex, goals to achieve and for which [the student] could make a conscious plan of attack" (Bloom & Broder, 1950, p. 8). Individually, students were given problems and then asked to "think aloud" as they worked through each problem. As a student thought aloud, an interviewer took as complete notes as possible on everything the student said and did. In certain cases, the interviewer asked students to recall what they had done while solving the problem after completing it.

The first study included twelve students, six of whom were academically successful (i.e., had high test scores and high grades) and six who were not. The purpose was to determine if there were differences in the problem-solving processes of the two groups. The researchers identified distinct differences in students' problem-solving processes:

- Understanding of the nature of problems
- Understanding of the ideas contained in problems
- General approach to the solution of problems
- Attitude toward solving problems

The second study examined differences in the problem-solving processes of students elicited by different types of problems. The researchers classified various problems according to their subject matter, their difficulty, and their format (e.g., true-false, multiple choice, constructed response). Common difficulties encountered by students attempting to solve the different types of problems were noted, as were difficulties associated with specific types of problems. These difficulties provided the basis for a series of recommendations concerning the improvement of test problems. In some cases, for example, the researchers minimized the use of relative terms in a problem, while in others they found it necessary to provide clearer directions.

The third study focused on students whose "failure on the comprehensive examinations might be due in large part to poor problem-solving methods" (Bloom & Broder, 1950, p. 67). The particular students selected for this investigation (1) had relatively high, scholastic aptitude test scores, especially considering their poor performance on the comprehensive examinations; (2) devoted at least an average amount of time to study; and (3) claimed that the examinations did not adequately reflect their understanding and mastery of the subject. The researchers in this study attempted to improve the problem-solving skills of these students and remedy their problem-solving deficiencies. A systematic approach to remediation was designed, implemented, and evaluated. Based on the results of the study, Bloom and Broder (1950) concluded, "the weight of the evidence is clearly that problem-solving remediation can help students" (p. 89). (See also Bloom, 1947.)

Problem-Solving Processes of College Students was a particularly significant book, especially considering when it was written. At the time, many cognitive skills, including problem-solving processes, were believed by most psychologists to be part of individuals' innate intelligence and relatively inalterable. Bloom and Broder showed, however, that not only could differences in college students' problem-solving processes be identified, but those processes could be improved through specific instructional strategies. In other words, such cognitive skills are, indeed, alterable.

In addition, the studies described in this book used data-gathering techniques quite unique for their time. Instead of observing overt behaviors, the dominant research methodology at the time, Bloom and Broder utilized students' self-reports of their mental processes during problem-solving tasks. Their methods not only laid the foundation for much of the cognitive research that would take place many years later and continues today, it also provided the basis for Ben's following work involving "stimulated recall." With this technique, instructors' presentations were recorded using audio recording equipment. Portions of the recording were then played back to students who were asked to recall what they were thinking about at that time (Bloom, 1953c, 1954b). Stimulated recall techniques allowed Ben and other researchers to gain insights into individuals' cognitive processes that could not be obtained through direct behavioral observations or other popular assessment techniques. They also became the foundation of cognitive research methodology for decades afterward. Even today, more than sixty years afterward, *Problem-Solving Processes of College Students* by Bloom and Broder is still cited in research studies and other works on cognitive processes, as evidenced in the following publications:

Beyer, B. K. (2008). What research tells us about teaching thinking skills. *The Social Studies, 99*(5), 223–232.

Jeffrey, L. M., Hide, S., & Lett, S. (2010). Learning characteristics of small business managers: Principles for training. *Journal of Workplace Learning, 22*(3), 146–165.

Koenig, R. (2010). *Learning for keeps: Teaching the strategies essential for creating independent learners.* Alexandria, VA: Association for Supervision and Curriculum Development.

Nickerson, R. S. (2010). *Mathematical reasoning: Patterns, problems, conjectures, and proofs.* New York, NY: Psychology Press, Taylor & Francis Group.

Stenning, K., & van Lambalgen, M. (2008). *Human reasoning and cognitive science.* Cambridge, MA: Massachusetts Institute of Technology Press.

Chapter 13

The Father of
Israeli Curriculum Reform

Shevach Eden

In the late 1950s the education system in Israel was subjected to the same harsh criticism as was levied against the U.S. education system. The success of the Soviet Union in launching the Sputnik satellite left many believing that both U.S. and Israeli schools were sorely lacking in most areas, especially in science and mathematics instruction. This criticism led to the appointment of commissions and task forces in both countries composed of leading scholars to develop plans for improving the quality and rigor of education programs.

In Israel a committee of eminent educators was assigned the task of developing plans to reform the educational system. After a year of work the committee published their recommendations, which called for only subtle, surface changes in the curriculum and in school organization. Dissatisfied with the committee's modest recommendations, the government chose not to implement the changes, despite the prestige of the committee's members.

Then in 1963, the Israeli Ministry of Education invited Ben to come to Israel as part of a United Nations Educational, Scientific, and Cultural Organization (UNESCO) project to advise ministry officials on implementing curriculum reform. Shevach Eden was appointed as Ben's liaison with the ministry during his stay, and provided the following story:

"At Ben's suggestion, I organized a seminar of successful teachers and outstanding scholars in each curriculum area. Those invited were asked to bring an outline of the objectives and learning goals for each area, along with samples of instructional materials they used to teach those objectives. Following the seminar Ben prepared a report for the ministry describing his views on what had been presented and what he believed would be necessary to achieve true reform. Specifically, he described the need for a major effort to devise new curricula focusing on the development of more complex cognitive skills and what he labeled 'higher mental processes.' He also emphasized the need to train curriculum experts who could take charge of this work in a national curriculum center. His report was enthusiastically received by both government officials and leaders in the Ministry of Education who hoped to move ahead immediately in implementing Ben's recommendations.

"To initiate his plan, Ben suggested to us that a group of ten outstanding teachers and scholars be sent to the University of Chicago for one year to participate in a special program he was organizing. According to Ben, this would provide them with the background and experiences they would need to accomplish these major curricula revisions. So the ministry developed selection criteria and chose a group of teachers and scholars to participate.

"After the group was named, however, several members of the selection committee expressed doubts about the skills of those who had been chosen. When efforts to resolve their disagreements failed, Ben was invited to return to Israel to advise in the selection process. He was, it seemed, the only person trusted by all parties involved in these disputes. So Ben came back to Israel and spent three days interviewing all of the candidates.

"At the end of his interviews Ben joined the skeptics in their assessment of the selected participants. He considered only half of the teachers and scholars chosen to be suitable for this important work. Ben then recommended that Israel's participation in the Chicago curriculum training program be postponed for one year and that the interim be spent in efforts to select a more qualified group of participants.

"Minister of Education Zalman Aran was greatly disappointed with Ben's appraisal of the selected candidates and with Ben's recommendation because it delayed plans for the needed curriculum reforms. New waves of immigrants who were less schooled than previous groups were flooding into Israel, and a significant educational gap was evident. School reform, based on significant revisions in curricula and considerable teacher training, was considered imperative in addressing this problem. Delaying participation in the Chicago program would mean postponing improvement efforts. Minister Aran therefore pressed Ben to reconsider his recommendation and to admit the educators chosen by the selection committee, indicating to Ben that these were the best that could be found.

"Ben, however, could not be budged and remained adamant in his decision. He pointed out that Professor Patenkin, head of the Department of Economics in Israel, had been sending two students each year to the University of Chicago for special training in economic development, and that these individuals had been exceptional students. Minister Aran countered that the most able students in Israel did not choose to study education. But again, Ben disagreed. He pointed out that several of his past doctoral students were from Israel and that they all were exceptionally bright, insightful, and talented. His hope was to work with more students of their caliber.

"After much debate, Minister Aran yielded to Ben's request. By that time I had developed a close friendship with Ben and was designated director of planning for the curriculum reform effort. I left for Chicago immediately to spend an academic quarter studying with Ben and becoming familiar with the demands of the University of Chicago. Upon my return to Israel, I organized a new selection committee that completed the task of choosing a new group of talented teachers and scholars. Together we traveled back to Chicago where we became immersed in theoretical and practical studies. Although all of us found the work to be extremely challenging, Ben was well pleased with our performance and told me that he held high hopes for what we might accomplish.

"Upon our return to Israel, our now close group of teachers and scholars formed a national Curriculum Center and began working on curricula reform. Ben kept close tabs on our work and remained a constant source of advice and encouragement. Despite numerous difficulties and setbacks, we made significant progress. The Curriculum Center grew in size and importance with affiliates established in many Israeli universities. Major conferences were held to acquaint Israeli educators with the new curricula, and programs and textbooks were published reflecting the changes. Ben was invited to speak at one of the conferences where he was hailed as the 'father of Israeli curriculum reform.' His influence on all that had been accomplished and his central role in the success of the reform effort was evident to everyone involved.

"When Ben organized the international seminar on curriculum construction in Gränna, Sweden, in 1971 involving representatives from twenty-three different countries, the leaders in the Israeli Curriculum Center were invited to present our work. In our presentation we stressed the vital importance of careful selection and high-quality training for those who would take responsibility for reform efforts. We also emphasized the importance of Ben's wise counsel, and stressed that his influence had been a key element in the Israeli success story.

"Since then curriculum reform efforts in Israel have continued. Even though Ben has not been directly involved in these efforts for many years, his influence stemming from those early reforms remains evident still today."

Chapter 14

An Itinerate Traveler

Richard Wolf

Richard Wolf was emeritus professor of education at Columbia University and a former student of Ben's. He also had the opportunity to travel with Ben on numerous occasions, mostly in connection with Ben's involvement in the International Association for the Evaluation of Educational Achievement (IEA). Ben was one of the first American educators to have a truly global view of education. He believed strongly that multinational studies of educational achievement would be highly informative to American educators and could spur improvements in our educational system. Following is Richard's story:

"Ben initially enlisted me to work with him on the first IEA study of mathematics achievement. It was anticipated that this first IEA study would involve testing roughly a quarter million students, and Ben believed that the only way that the study could be completed would be to use computers to analyze the resulting data. Since I was one of the few Chicago students who had worked with computers at that time, Ben felt that I was the best prepared to take on this huge data analysis task. I, more out of youthful enthusiasm than wisdom, eagerly accepted Ben's invitation.

"One of the first meetings of the group that would plan and conduct the study took place in Hamburg, Germany, in September 1963. Ben felt that it was important for me to attend that meeting to get a better sense of the work and the project's goals. At that time, however, I had never traveled abroad and was quite apprehensive about the trip. But with Ben's assurance, I obtained a passport, purchased the airline ticket, and was ready to go.

"When we arrived in Hamburg, I found it to be, in William James's words, '. . . a blooming, buzzing confusion.' Not knowing the language or much about our surroundings, I felt completely lost. Ben immediately sensed my bewilderment and took me under his wing. He assisted me in checking into the hotel and was never far from my side throughout the entire week we spent in Hamburg. Perhaps it is more accurate to say that I never strayed far from Ben's side because of the uncertainty and disorientation I felt.

"Although in my confusion I was not fully aware of it at the time, this was a crucial meeting for Ben. IEA was still a fledgling organization with a fragile structure and uncertain future. Ben understood that realizing his dream of a worldwide effort to gather information on student achievement in mathematics rested on the cooperation and support of the educational leaders assembled in Hamburg. He also knew that gaining their cooperation and support would require constant attention, sensitive negotiation, and diplomatic skill.

"Despite these demands, however, Ben made persistent efforts to ensure my welfare, treating me more like a young son than a naïve graduate student. He went out of his way to help me develop confidence and certainty in this new and unfamiliar professional environment. His kindness and caring at this crucial time showed me a personal side of Ben that those who knew him only as a scholar and researcher would never see.

"At these meetings in Hamburg, I sat with people I knew only by their outstanding reputations and, of course, from the research literature in education. Torsten Husén of Sweden chaired the meetings. Other notable attendees included Robert Thorndike of Teachers College, Columbia University; Douglas Pidgeon of England; Gaston Mialaret of France; Martti Takala of Finland; and Gilbert Peaker of England. I also met Neville Postlethwaite, the administrator of the study, who would become one of my closest friends. The work was intense and exhausting, but Ben carefully shepherded me through the meetings with patience and grace.

"The only downside I discovered to traveling with Ben was mealtime. While engaged in these intense work sessions, Ben had little or no interest in food. Meals were part extension of the work and part seminar, typically conducted by Ben. So intent was his focus on the goals of our meeting that participants often expressed surprise that Ben actually found time to eat anything.

"The sole embarrassing moment for me came when the group would finally end our work sessions and order food. If Ben ordered meat, he carefully instructed the waiter that it must be 'well done,' usually adding, 'I don't want to recognize the beast!' Waiters often tried to convince him otherwise, but Ben was adamant, frequently pointing out that it was he who would be eating the dinner, not the waiter. As one who was reared on ordering steaks medium rare, I found this a bit awkward, especially in elegant German restaurants.

"The 1963 Hamburg trip was the first of several that Ben and I took together. Our other trips took us to Stockholm, London, Honolulu, Paris, and Toronto, as well as New York and Los Angeles. On all occasions Ben's kindness to me was unwavering. His caring and nurturing way made a lasting impression that I cherished through all the days of my professional career and profoundly affected the way I interacted with my own graduate students. He was a man of amazing talent and uncommon humanity."

Chapter 15

A Constant Encourager

Leah Shefatya

Throughout his career Ben shared a close relationship with educators in Israel. One of his earliest visits came in 1963 when he traveled to Israel at the request of the Israeli Ministry of Education. In addition to consulting on several ministry programs, Ben used the visit to encourage the participation of ministry officials in a special yearlong seminar on curriculum planning that he was organizing at the University of Chicago.

Much of his time in Israel was spent at the Henrietta Szold Institute for Research in the Behavioral Sciences in Jerusalem. Institute director Moshe Smilansky was a great admirer of Ben's work and took the opportunity to have Ben join in discussions with the institute staff about their current and planned research projects. Staff members were quite taken by Ben and stayed long after their normal working hours in order to join him in conversation. Not only were they impressed with his expertise and the insights he offered on every topic discussed, but also with his unpretentious manner and friendly style. They were amazed to find this famous American educator so congenial and approachable.

One institute staff member especially impressed by Ben was Leah Shefatya, who at that time was working with Sarah Smilansky on early childhood projects. Leah and her colleagues were quite taken by Ben's enormous pride in the University of Chicago as an institution of higher education. In nearly every conversation Ben emphasized the outstanding reputation of the Chicago faculty and the many unique programs the university offered. They were also surprised, however, to find him so modest about his own accomplishments, which at the time were already considerable. They all had been required to read the work of Benjamin Bloom in their education classes and frequently cited his articles and books in their own research.

42

Leah provided the following story of her experiences with Ben:

"The year after I met Mr. Bloom during one of his many visits to Israel, my husband was sent to Chicago by the Jewish Agency to serve for two years as the facilitator for immigration to Israel in the midwestern United States. On learning of our move, Mr. Bloom and his wife, Sophie, went out of their way to ensure a smooth transition to the United States for our family, including our three young daughters. After we were settled in Chicago, we became regular visitors in the Blooms' home, and our two families soon became close friends.

"A short time later Szold Institute director Moshe Smilansky earned a sabbatical to study at the University of Chicago, and Mr. Bloom asked me if I would help select an apartment for him and his family. During our search together, Mr. Bloom questioned me about my own plans for the upcoming two years. Surprised by his inquiry, I indicated that I really had no professional plans at all. I believed that my role was primarily to take care of our family and to help them adjust to our new environment in the United States. Mr. Bloom acknowledged the importance of that responsibility, but suggested that I might also benefit from graduate work in the Department of Education.

"So after the Smilanskys arrived and were settled, and I made suitable arrangements for my daughters, I took Mr. Bloom's advice and registered for a single course during the winter quarter at the University of Chicago. The work proved demanding both intellectually and practically, but the experience was exceptionally exciting. So the following spring quarter I made plans to enroll in two courses. After reviewing our family's financial situation, however, it became apparent that the cost would be too great, and I considered canceling my plans. When Mr. Bloom learned of this, he made special arrangements to help me obtain a tuition scholarship that allowed me to continue my studies.

"Mr. Bloom kept close tabs on my academic progress and took great pride in my successes. One day while I was having lunch at a cafeteria on campus, he came from across the room to tell me that Professor Jacob Getzels, the eminent educational psychologist in whose seminar I was enrolled, thought quite highly of my work and my contributions in class. I thanked him, of course, but considered the compliment nothing more than his fatherly attempt to encourage my continued hard work. Noting my unenthusiastic response, Mr. Bloom continued, 'No, you don't understand. Getzels rarely offers compliments.'

"I completed the coursework for my doctorate and eventually set to the task of preparing my dissertation proposal under Mr. Bloom's supervision. For weeks I worked to develop a draft version of a proposal that I submitted to Mr. Bloom for his review. It was thorough, detailed, and centered on issues that I believed held great significance.

"The meeting with Mr. Bloom to discuss my draft did not go at all as I expected, however. He had crossed out large portions of the text on nearly every page of the draft. He wanted me to cut major components of what I had outlined and concentrate on a much narrower set of questions. As I looked over the draft, I was convinced that he must have been very disappointed with my work. But during our discussion, Mr. Bloom clarified his perspective and the reasons for his harsh editing.

"'Leah, do you want to finish your dissertation before you leave?' he asked.

"'But of course, Mr. Bloom,' I replied. 'That's always been my plan.'

"'In that case,' he said, holding up my draft, 'you must narrow your focus. I recommend that you cut this, and this, and this. . . .'

"'But Mr. Bloom,' I responded, 'these are important issues. This is what fascinates me. This is what I want to understand better. I believe these are important questions worthy of investigation.'

"Mr. Bloom smiled and sat back in his chair. 'I agree with you, Leah,' he began. 'But you have all your life ahead of you to find the answers to questions you consider important. You don't have to include them *all* in your dissertation.'

"His point was clear. To Mr. Bloom, the doctoral dissertation was only the beginning of a career in research, and a modest beginning at that. It was an initial foray into an exciting and challenging area that held great interest for a student. It laid the foundation from which new and even better work would come. So I refined my proposal, completed my doctoral dissertation, and went on to a highly productive career as a researcher at the Szold Institute in Israel."

Chapter 16

Taxonomy of Educational Objectives, Handbook 1: The Cognitive Domain

Thomas R. Guskey

The work for which Ben is undoubtedly most recognized is his leadership in the development of the *Taxonomy of Educational Objectives, Handbook 1: The Cognitive Domain* (Bloom, Engelhart, Furst, Hill, & Krathwohl, 1956). When originally published in 1956, the *Taxonomy* received scant attention from researchers or practitioners. Few thought it was very important. Not until nearly a decade later did it capture the attention of educators at all levels and serve as the foundation for curriculum restructuring efforts throughout the United States and around the world.

"Bloom's *Taxonomy*," as it came to be known, has been translated into more than twenty different languages and remains one of the most widely distributed and best-known books in all of education. Ben always claimed, however, that the *Taxonomy* was "one of the most widely cited yet least read books in American education" (Anderson and Sosniak, 1994). Even today, more than fifty years after its original publication, beginning teachers everywhere still commit to memory its six major levels: knowledge, comprehension, application, analysis, synthesis, and evaluation.

The *Taxonomy* grew from Ben's work in the University of Chicago's Board of Examinations office and from the influence of Ralph Tyler. In the model that he devised for curriculum development and then extended to program evaluation, Tyler (1942) stressed that an essential first step is clarification of the program or activity's goals. With goals clearly specified, efforts can then focus on the extent to which those goals were achieved. As Tyler (1949) put it:

If an educational program is to be planned and if efforts for continued improvement are to be made, it is necessary to have some conception of the goals that are
being sought. These educational objectives become the criteria by which materials are selected, content is outlined, instructional procedures are developed and
tests and examinations are prepared. All aspects of the educational program are
really means to accomplish these basic educational purposes. (p. 3)

Although Tyler believed that well-defined goals and objectives should drive
curriculum development and evaluation procedures, he also emphasized
that educators must continually reexamine the importance and meaning of
the goals they set. Tyler further noted that a thorough examination of potential goals and objectives inevitably comes down to questions about what is
most valued by the organization or the individuals involved. He stressed:

In the final analysis, objectives are matters of choice, and they must therefore be considered value judgments of those responsible for the school. A
comprehensive philosophy of education is necessary to guide one in making
these judgments. In addition, certain kinds of information and knowledge
provide a more intelligent basis for applying the philosophy in making decisions about objectives. If these facts are available to those making decisions,
the probability is increased that judgments about objectives will have greater
significance and greater validity. (Tyler, 1949, p. 4)

Tyler's model brought clarity, order, direction, and objectivity to curriculum development and evaluation—qualities that were generally lacking
in these endeavors prior to Tyler's work. But as educators began clarify-
ing their goals and objectives for student learning, another problem became evident: the goals and objectives they identified varied widely. Most
were relatively simple and required only that students recall factual information. Others were much more complex, requiring students to engage in
more sophisticated forms of reasoning, problem solving, and other higher
mental processes. While these differences were generally recognized, no
procedures existed for ordering or classifying them.

This was the task that Ben and his colleagues set out to accomplish in
developing the *Taxonomy*. They wanted to develop a conceptual framework that would bring a sense of order to this variation in the cognitive
complexity of the goals and objectives of education. As they emphasized
in their introduction to the *Taxonomy*:

You are reading about an attempt to build a taxonomy of educational objectives. It is intended to provide for classification of the goals of our educational system. It is expected to be of general help to all teachers, administrators, professional specialists, and research workers who deal with curricular
and evaluation problems. It is especially intended to help them discuss these
problems with greater precision. (Bloom et al., 1956, p. 1)

From the very beginning, Ben had high hopes for what such a taxonomy might bring. At the Allerton Conference, the first conference devoted to the work he and his colleagues were about to take on in developing the *Taxonomy* (Krathwohl, 1994), Ben began by describing his vision for the project. He hoped their work might result in an empirically built "examiners' taxonomy," designed to facilitate the development, classification, and exchange of test questions—an early approach to item banking. But he ended his presentation with an even bolder challenge:

> There is a larger task that we may wish to consider. . . . A taxonomy of educational outcomes could do much to bring order out of chaos in the field of education. It could furnish the conceptual framework around which our descriptions of educational programs and experiences could be oriented. It could furnish a framework for the development of educational theories and research. It could furnish the scheme needed for training our teachers and for orienting them to the varied possibilities of education. (Bloom, 1949, cited in Krathwohl, 1994, p. 181)

Ben and his colleagues first discussed the idea of a taxonomy at an informal meeting of college and university examiners attending the 1948 American Psychological Association convention in Boston. Their original plans called for a complete taxonomy in three parts: the cognitive, affective, and psychomotor domains. They decided to start with the cognitive domain, however, because it was most central to curriculum development and test development at the time.

Five guiding principles were established for their work. First, they believed that a taxonomy should focus on intended learning outcomes rather than student learning processes. In other words, it should center on what educators want students to learn and be able to do, not on how students achieve those goals. Second, the major distinctions among the taxonomic categories should reflect the distinctions that teachers make among them. Third, a taxonomy should be "logically developed and internally consistent." Fourth, a taxonomy should be consistent with "our present understanding of psychological phenomena." And fifth, the classification should be purely descriptive, in contrast to value oriented, so that every type of educational goal would "fit" somewhere (Bloom, et al., 1956, p. 14).

Even with these guiding principles set forth, however, development was not easy. The name "taxonomy" itself proved controversial. As Ben later related:

> The committee that met to develop the *Taxonomy* initially disputed the use of the term "taxonomy." However, I believed that the term was quite distinctive and descriptive. Eventually, the committee agreed that the term would

be used and it has become commonplace not only in education but in other fields as well. (Bloom, 1994, p. 1)

With their guiding principles established, committee members identified the familiar set of six levels or categories: knowledge, comprehension, application, analysis, synthesis, and evaluation. These categories were presumed to exist along a continuum of cognitive complexity and difficulty, with each higher level building on and incorporating the lower ones. Ben and his colleagues emphasized, however, that this hierarchy was not perfect and numerous exceptions exist for both curriculum development and evaluation. They also stressed that while higher-level objectives were undoubtedly more difficult for teachers to teach and for students to learn, they were more likely to be retained by students for longer periods of time. For example, while most adults can apply their knowledge of subtraction to common mathematics problems, few are likely to recall which term in a subtraction problem is the "subtrahend" and which is the "minuend."

The *Taxonomy* had a profound influence on education and educators. One of the most important was to provide a panorama of educational goals much broader than might otherwise have been considered (Krathwohl, 1994). The *Taxonomy* showed educators the multitude of important learning outcomes that extend far beyond recall of basic information and pressed them to consider these more complex goals. As such, it offered "easily understandable guidelines for expanding both curriculum and evaluation beyond simple knowledge" (Postlethwaite, 1994, p. 179).

Ben emphasized this same contribution years later when he wrote:

> The phenomenal growth of the use of the *Taxonomy* can only be explained by the fact that it filled a void; it met a previously unmet need for basic, fundamental planning in education. For the first time, educators were able to evaluate the learning of students systematically. As they did so, they became aware that too much emphasis was being placed on the lowest level of the *Taxonomy*: Knowledge. Frequently as much as 90 percent of instructional time was spent at this level, with very little time spent on the higher mental processes that would enable students to apply their knowledge creatively. With the explosion of knowledge that has taken place during the past forty years, the ability to use higher mental processes has assumed prime importance. (Bloom, 1994, p. 1)

While the *Taxonomy*'s impact in the United States was great, it was perhaps even greater internationally (Anderson, 1994; Sosniak, 1994). In numerous countries around the world, the *Taxonomy* served as the basis for curriculum development and reform, test construction, lesson planning, and teacher training (Chung, 1994; Lewy & Báthory, 1994). In 1986, for example, Ben was invited by Lin Fu Nian, honorary president of East China Normal University in Shanghai, to be an exchange scholar. One of his primary responsibilities there was to conduct a series of seminars in which he described and discussed the *Taxonomy*. Lin Fu Nian was so impressed with Ben's description that he had the *Taxonomy* translated into Chinese and distributed a million copies to educators throughout China. The magnitude of this effort is truly mind-boggling (Bloom, 1994).

The *Taxonomy* also provided the basis for the *Handbook on Formative and Summative Evaluation of Student Learning* (Bloom, Hastings, & Madaus, 1971), which "brought together the best techniques available for evaluating the *improvement* of student learning" (Bloom, 1994, p. 5). The major assumption of this volume is that "education must be increasingly concerned about the fullest development of *all* children and youth, and it will be the responsibility of the schools to seek learning conditions which will enable each individual to reach the highest level of learning possible" (Bloom, et al., 1971, p. 6). This, in turn, provided the foundation for what would eventually become *All Our Children Learning* (Bloom, 1981a).

In addition, the popularity and practical utility of the *Taxonomy* provided the impetus for educational leaders from around the world to become involved in collaborative curriculum restructuring efforts initiated at the Gränna (Sweden) Conference in 1971. This unprecedented event in international collaboration brought together curriculum specialists from twenty-three different countries located on five continents: Africa, Asia, Europe, and North and South America. It also laid the foundation for a series of international comparisons of student achievement coordinated through the International Association for the Evaluation of Educational Achievement (IEA).

Like any major work, however, the *Taxonomy* was not without its critics. The criticisms of the *Taxonomy* range from its neglect of educational goals that do not lend themselves to precise specification, to the exclusive focus on cognitive processes at the expense of content, and to the validity of the assumption of a cumulative hierarchy (see Furst, 1994, for a useful summary). Remarkably, nearly all of these criticisms were both anticipated and addressed by Ben and his colleagues in their original description of the *Taxonomy*, though not to the satisfaction of some. As Ben noted:

> The *Taxonomy* does not impose a set of teaching procedures, nor does it view objectives as so detailed and restrictive that a single teaching method is implied. . . . [It] does imply the need for teachers to help students learn to apply their knowledge to problems arising in their own experiences and to be able to deal effectively with problems that are not familiar to them. This emphasis alone should guard against the rote learning of ready-made solutions. It is

obvious, at least to me, that many of the criticisms directed toward the *Tax-onomy* have resulted from very narrow interpretations of both the *Taxonomy* and its proper application. (Bloom, 1994, p. 7)

Over the years different authors have published several revisions and adaptations of the *Taxonomy*, each offering a slightly different perspective on how best to organize and classify educational goals and objectives. The better known among these include Anderson and Krathwohl's *A Tax-onomy for Learning, Teaching, and Assessing* (2001) and Marzano's *Designing a New Taxonomy of Educational Objectives* (2001). While thoughtfully conceived and useful in many contexts, it seems unlikely these revisions will ever reach the prominence of the original *Taxonomy* in the United States or internationally.

It would be difficult to find another, single publication in all of education that has had a more powerful and sustained influence on education theory and practice than "Bloom's *Taxonomy*." Since its publication in 1956, citation indices show that it has been referenced in books, articles, dissertations, and theses more than sixteen thousand times. And there is no indication that influence is diminishing. Since 2010, the *Taxonomy of Educational Objectives, Handbook 1: The Cognitive Domain* has been cited in more than a thousand publications, including the following examples:

Arends, R. I., & Kilcher, A. (2010). *Teaching for student learning: Becoming an accomplished teacher.* New York, NY: Routledge.

Morrow, J. R., Jackson, J. W., Disch, J. G., & Mood, D. P. (2010). *Measurement and evaluation in human performance* (4th ed.). Champaign, IL: Human Kinetics.

Novak, J. D. (2010). *Learning, creating, and using knowledge: Concept maps as facilitative tools in schools and corporations* (2nd ed.). New York, NY: Routledge.

Powell, R. G., & Powell, D. L. (2010). *Classroom communication and diversity: Enhancing instructional practice* (2nd ed.). New York, NY: Routledge.

Wiggins, G., & McTighe, J. (2011). *The understanding by design guide to creating high quality units.* Alexandria, VA: Association for Supervision and Curriculum Development.

Chapter 17

The Origins of the *Taxonomy*

Edward Kifer

As lead author of the *Taxonomy of Educational Objectives, Handbook 1: The Cognitive Domain* (Bloom, Engelhart, Furst, Hill, & Krathwohl, 1956), Ben gained widespread recognition and fame. This simple but elegant guide became the basis of curriculum development work throughout the world and in many circles came to be known simply as "Bloom's *Taxonomy*." In discussing this work, however, Ben always stressed that the ideas behind the *Taxonomy* had a long history in education and did not originate with the group of university examiners that assembled it. Edward (Skip) Kifer, emeritus professor of education at the University of Kentucky and former student of Ben's, shared the following story that further emphasizes Ben's point:

"With Ben's assistance and support, I won a Spencer Foundation Post-Doctoral Fellowship that allowed me to spend a year in Stockholm, Sweden, working at an educational institute headed by Torsten Husén. While there I participated on a panel of academics from the United States, one of whom was studying the history of literacy in Sweden.

"The Swedes were literate long before they had a system of formal public education. As a product of the Reformation and a Lutheran dictate to have the Bible in the vernacular, parish ministers in Sweden were expected to teach their parishioners how to read. The minister would choose one person in each family to teach to read, and then that person was expected to teach others.

"I found many aspects of this project fascinating, not the least of which was how the parish minister evaluated the readers. If the person were able to read the words in the Bible, they received a vertical line indicating such. If they could put what they read into their own words, a horizontal

51

line was added to the vertical one. Finally, if the reader could take the moral lesson in the reading passage and apply it to everyday life, the person received another vertical mark, completing an inverted 'U' and indicating he or she was now considered literate.

"Upon returning from Sweden, I was having dinner with Ben one evening and told him about the project. As I concluded my story, I mentioned to Ben how similar the Swedes' categories were to the first three levels of the *Taxonomy*—they looked to me very much like knowledge, comprehension, and application.

"Ben's reaction was modest and direct. He simply smiled and said to me, 'Where do you think we got the idea?' Hence, it seems that all of us 'borrow' great ideas from time to time."

Chapter 18

Ideas Ahead of Their Time

Peter Airasian

Albert Szent-Gyorgyi once remarked, "Research is to see what everybody else has seen, and to think what no one else has thought." No researcher in the field of education exemplified this better than Benjamin Bloom. His keen perception and creative approach to educational problems led him to see things differently than did others in the field and, as a result, to develop ideas that were truly ahead of their time. On numerous occasions throughout his long career, Ben explored topics and provided insights into critical issues in education long before their importance became apparent to the mainstream of educational researchers.

Today, perhaps due to carelessness in reviewing the research literature, modern scholars frequently go about their work unaware of these significant contributions. As a result, they conduct investigations that "rediscover" what Ben found years earlier, rarely acknowledging his contribution or giving credit to his pioneering work. Peter Airasian, former professor of education at Boston College and a former student of Ben's, shared the following experience to illustrate this point:

"In 1961, Ben and Frank Peters wrote a book entitled *Use of Academic Prediction Scales for Counseling and Selecting College Entrants* (Bloom & Peters, 1961). The research they described took a logical and simple approach to improving prediction scales for college admission. Instead of using only high school grade point average (GPA) as a predictor of college success, Bloom and Peters crossed GPA with the difficulty level of students' high school curriculum. Taking these two predictors significantly improved the selection of first-year college success in a logical and commonsensical way.

"Six years after publication of Bloom and Peters' book, a prominent researcher from the Educational Testing Service (ETS) was invited to present the 'newest' research on improving prediction scales for college admission to a MESA (Measurement, Evaluation, and Statistical Analysis) seminar at the University of Chicago. For an hour and a half the presenter filled the blackboard with symbols, equations, diagrams, and statistics. Most of us students and several of the faculty members in attendance had difficulty following the presentation, but that did not seem to deter the presenter who continued without pause. When the seminar ended, everyone left with careful notes on the complex but obscure explanations. We also left wondering why Ben's related and seemingly more elegant research, with which we were all familiar, was never mentioned.

"More recently, a widely publicized study sponsored by the Office of Educational Research and Improvement in the U.S. Department of Education once again rediscovered what Bloom and Peters described nearly forty years earlier. Charles Adelman (1999) found that an index of the rigor of students' high school curriculum, composed of the number of Advanced Placement courses taken, the highest level of math studied, and total number of courses completed, was a much stronger predictor of college success than standardized test scores, grade point average, or class rank. As Yogi Berra once remarked, 'It's *deja vu* all over again!'"

Chapter 19

A Powerful Influence in Africa

Christopher Modu

Ben's role in the development of curricula and assessment programs in developed countries throughout the world is fairly well documented. But few people know about his extensive work in third world nations, particularly in Africa. Christopher Modu, former chief-of-party for the World Bank Education Project in Liberia, former associate director of the Statistical Analysis Division at the Educational Testing Service, and former student of Ben's, witnessed much of this work firsthand. He offered the following story:

"My association with Mr. Bloom began in 1961 when, as a member of the West African Examinations Council, I arrived at the University of Chicago on Ford Foundation scholarships to work for a year on the development of international secondary school graduation examinations in West Africa. Mr. Bloom guided our work for the entire year, helping our team to accomplish more than anyone expected. To everyone in our group he became a mentor and friend, frequently inviting us and the other members of our families to join him and Sophie in their home for dinner. Mr. Bloom's warm hospitality and Sophie's graciousness made lasting impressions on all.

"After returning to Africa, I continued to work with Mr. Bloom through my participation in the African Mathematics Program for seven consecutive summers beginning in 1962. This program, sponsored by the United States Agency for International Development (USAID) and other U.S. philanthropic foundations, involved the development in East Africa of a series of modern mathematics textbooks and corresponding teachers' guides for use in elementary and secondary schools throughout English-speaking African countries. Like the other African projects to which Mr. Bloom contributed, this program was a remarkable success.

"My dream to return to the University of Chicago to complete my doctoral degree in the Measurement, Evaluation, and Statistical Analysis (MESA) Program under Mr. Bloom's direction was realized in 1967. But my three years as a student at the university proved more challenging than I ever expected. Because of a bitter civil war in Nigeria, I frequently lost all contact with members of my family, who were completely cut off in the eastern part of that country. Were it not for Mr. Bloom's guidance, understanding, and friendship during this trying time, I doubt I would have been able to endure the experience or to complete my degree.

"The difference that Mr. Bloom made in my life was immense. And despite all that he gave, Mr. Bloom never expected anything in return. He shunned even my most modest efforts to do things for him. His only expectation was that the same level of guidance and support that he offered be extended by his students to others."

Chapter 20

Stability and Change in Human Characteristics

Thomas R. Guskey

During his first fifteen years as a faculty member in the University of Chicago's Department of Education, Ben's writings reflected primarily his work with the Board of Examinations and the strong influence of his mentor, Ralph W. Tyler (e.g., Bloom, 1957, 1958a, 1958b; Bloom & Heyns, 1956; Bloom & Statler, 1957; Bloom & Webster, 1960). But in 1959, on Tyler's recommendation, Ben left his position as university examiner and spent a year at the Center for Advanced Study in Behavioral Sciences in Stanford, California. The center was established to give promising scholars the opportunity to develop their research interests more fully, in collaboration with other scholars and unencumbered by tangential professional responsibilities.

The experience at the center marked a significant turning point in Ben's research and writing. His intellectual focus shifted from problems in testing, measurement, and evaluation, to problems in learning (e.g., Bloom, 1966a, 1974b), human development (Bloom, 1973, 1985), curriculum (Bloom, 1965a, 1974a), instruction (Bloom, 1968a, 1984b), and educational research (Bloom, 1966c, 1980). It was also at this time that Ben established his true independence as a scholar and researcher, stepping out of, and in many ways beyond, the shadow of Ralph Tyler.

During his stay at the center, Ben began work on what would become *Stability and Change in Human Characteristics* (Bloom, 1964). In his words:

The freedom from the usual schedule and duties, the opportunity to explore a problem as deeply as possible, and the encouragement of the staff and other Fellows did much to help me get started on the problem of stability and change. The major outline of [the book] was completed at the Center. (p. ix)

In developing *Stability and Change,* Ben returned to his roots as a psychologist. It was the first of several of his major explorations into the nature of human development and the alterability of human characteristics. As he described in the book's first chapter:

> This book . . . represents an attempt to identify "stable" [human] characteristics, to describe the extent to which such characteristics are stabilized at various ages, and to determine the conditions under which this stability may be modified. Hopefully, this work will enable us to understand how such characteristics may be identified, explained, and, eventually, modified. (Bloom, 1964, p. 2)

To accomplish this purpose Ben gathered and summarized the results of longitudinal studies pertaining to three sets of human attributes: physical (e.g., height, weight, and strength), cognitive (e.g., intelligence and school achievement), and affective (e.g., interests, attitudes, and personality). A single mathematical formula $[I_2 = I_1 + f (E_{2-1})]$ was used to frame his analysis of the data and to guide his interpretation of the results. In the formula I_1 and I_2 stand for measures of a characteristic at two points in time. E_{2-1} represents relevant environmental factors that were in place during the interim. In words, the formula suggests that a person's height (or intelligence or interests) at one point in time is attributable to some combination of the person's height (or intelligence or interests) at some earlier time and the environmental conditions he or she experienced during the intervening years.

Crucial to understanding Ben's findings and conclusions in *Stability* is his definition of a "stable" characteristic:

> Empirically, a stable characteristic is one that is consistent from one point in time to another. If pressed, one might further delimit this by specifying the time intervals as one year or more and the minimum level of consistency as a correlation of +.50 or higher. Defined in this way, a stable characteristic may be one that is different quantitatively as well as qualitatively at the two time points if the change is predictable to some minimal degree. (Bloom, 1964, p. 3)

Thus, Ben saw stability as relative, not absolute. He illustrated his definition of stability using the characteristic of "height":

> A good illustration of a stable characteristic from this point of view is height, which changes from birth to maturity, and yet height at maturity is highly predictable from height at ages three or four. That is, the *relative* height positions of a sample of boys or girls are highly consistent from one age to another. (p. 3)

Richard Wolf, former emeritus professor at Columbia University and a former student of Ben's, worked closely with Ben while he was developing *Stability*. Richard notes that Ben used the term "constancy" to refer to absolute stability and the term "consistency" to refer to relative stability. Ben made special mention of Richard's contribution to this work in the preface to *Stability and Change*. There Ben noted: "Dr. Wolf, in particular, has contributed to this work to such a level that I have difficulty at present in differentiating his work and ideas from my own" (Bloom, 1964, p. ix).

According to the data Ben summarized, all of the characteristics examined achieved a reasonable degree of stability by age eight, with most stabilizing between ages three and four. In addition, he also found that in most of the characteristics studied there was an initial period of relatively rapid change followed by an extended period of relatively slow change. This led him to make what is perhaps the most frequently quoted statement from the book: "With the exception of school achievement, the most rapid period for . . . development . . . is in the first five years of life" (p. 204).

Based on these data, Ben suggested that the power of environmental factors to influence change in human characteristics decreases as the characteristics become more stable. With respect to intelligence, for example, he asserted that "marked changes in the environment in the early years can produce greater changes in intelligence than will equally marked changes in the environment at later periods of development" (p. 89).

To Ben, the implications of these findings for education were clear. He interpreted the results pertaining to school achievement as suggesting "the great importance of the first few years of school as well as the preschool period in . . . developing . . . learning patterns and general achievement" (p. 127). In other words, education's greatest potential influence was clearly in the earliest years.

Prior to the publication of *Stability*, but armed with his results and supporting data, Ben testified before Congress as legislators debated the structure and merits of the Economic Opportunity Act (EOA), one of the cornerstones of President Lyndon Johnson's "Great Society" legislation. In its final form, the EOA contained funding for the early childhood education program, Head Start, much due to the influence of Ben's work.

When Ben passed away in September 1999, the writers of two of his obituaries emphasized his role in the creation of Head Start (Honan, 1999; Woo, 1999). Honan, in fact, who prepared the obituary for the *New York Times*, referred to *Stability and Change in Human Characteristics* as Ben's "most influential book." Still today, *Stability and Change* continues to be cited in books and research articles as a hallmark work in human development and early childhood education, including the following examples:

Hardman, M. L., Drew, C. J., & Egan, W. (2010). *Human exceptionality: School, community, and family* (10th ed.). Belmont, CA: Wadsworth, Cengage Learning.

Karch, A. (2010). Policy feedback and preschool finding in the American states. *Policy Studies Journal, 38*(2), 217–234.

Miller, D. F. (2010). *Positive child guidance* (6th ed.). Belmont, CA: Wadsworth, Cengage Learning.

Phillips, D. A., & Lowenstein, A. E. (2011). Early care, education, and child development. *Annual Review of Psychology, 62*, 483–500.

Sternberg, R. J., Jarvin, L., & Grigorenko, E. L. (2011). *Explorations in giftedness.* New York, NY: Cambridge University Press.

Chapter 21

Multiple Approaches and Tenacity

Richard Wolf

Ben had a number of distinctive qualities that contributed to his uniqueness as a researcher. According to Richard Wolf, emeritus professor of education at Columbia University and a former student of Ben's, two of those qualities were his ability to approach a problem from a variety of perspectives and his unrelenting tenacity. Ben viewed problems from every point of view he could imagine and pursued solutions to those problems with boundless energy. A dramatic illustration of these qualities occurred while Richard was serving as Ben's research assistant from 1961 to 1963, when Ben was working on *Stability and Change in Human Characteristics* (Bloom, 1964). Ben and Richard worked almost every day on the book and often over weekends. Richard described the experience in this way:

"One Friday, Ben asked me if I would mind coming in on Saturday so that we could continue work on a particularly challenging aspect of the project. We were trying to estimate environmental effects from Newman, Freeman, and Holzinger's book, *Twins: A Study of Heredity and Environment*. Although published in 1937, Ben believed the book never received the attention it deserved. The authors had identified nineteen pairs of identical twins that had been separated at birth and raised in different home settings. The first part of the book was devoted largely to establishing the monozygoticity of the twins, a necessary prerequisite to any further work with the data. The investigators then collected copious amounts of information on the characteristics of the twin pairs (physical, intellectual, achievement, and personality data). Our task in analyzing their work was to estimate the effects of the home environments on the characteristics of the subjects. Fortunately for us, the book contained virtually all the raw data on the members of the twin pairs.

"We started early that Saturday morning, trying one approach after another to estimate the effects of home environments on the characteristics of the subjects. But time after time, each approach failed. Although we found consistent evidence of environmental effects, our estimates of the magnitude of these effects were generally smaller than what Ben thought they should be. By mid-afternoon, I had grown frustrated and discouraged, and doubted we would find anything substantial in the way of environmental effects. Ben, however, was not deterred.

"Finally late in the afternoon, after numerous unsuccessful attempts, we hit on the idea of relating differences in the measured intelligence of the twin pairs to differences in the ratings of the intellectual environments in which they were raised. I was not particularly enthusiastic about this approach since I was aware of the unreliability of difference scores. Ben, on the other hand, remained upbeat and optimistic about finding large home environment effects.

"Initially we used a tetrachoric approach to estimate the correlation between the two sets of differences and found a substantial correlation. But Ben had doubts about the crudeness of tetrachoric correlations, and insisted that we compute a Pearson correlation coefficient between the two sets of difference scores. I completed the calculations and obtained a correlation coefficient of +.80. Ben was greatly pleased. So at five o'clock, after nine hours of steady work on the project, he announced that we had done a good day's work and could call it quits for the day. I was exhausted. Ben, on the other hand, was exhilarated and seemed to have more energy than when we began our day together.

"That Saturday taught me an important lesson. A less tenacious investigator would never have devoted that amount of time and effort to a single study. Ben kept coming up with one new approach after another in our search for home environment effects. In fact, it took the entire day. The payoff, however, was enormous. The results and discussion of the Newman, Freeman, and Holzinger book received considerable attention in *Stability and Change in Human Characteristics*. In addition, the work that Ben and I did that day led directly to my dissertation research, in which I developed a new approach to measuring home environment effects on intelligence. Our work together on that long Saturday, grueling as it was for me, was clearly the inspiration for my dissertation and for many projects afterward."

Chapter 22

On Publishing

Jeremy Finn

While Ben frequently engaged students in his research projects, he also pressed them hard to develop their own ideas. He always insisted, however, that their research and writing address highly significant questions that intrigued them and to which they wanted to contribute new understanding. For Ben, writing was not done for the sake of publication, but to add something meaningful and important to the profession. Jeremy Finn, professor of education at the State University of New York at Buffalo and former student of Ben's, learned about this from Ben in a very poignant way:

"During my second year of study in the Measurement, Evaluation, and Statistical Analysis (MESA) Program, several of my fellow graduate students and I were discussing the importance of publishing in academic positions. We knew that the major research universities where we hoped one day to work considered publications to be extremely important. Yet in none of our classes or seminars had publishing ever been discussed. So I was nominated to approach Ben on behalf of the group to discuss the issue.

"After mustering my courage and carefully preparing my approach, I went to Ben with my question. Despite the seriousness of my tone, however, Ben seemed indifferent to the issue. A bit frustrated his lack of response, I pressed harder. 'Julian Stanley at the University of Wisconsin is encouraging his students to publish articles, both with him and on their own, while they are in graduate school,' I said. 'It seems to us that they will have a real advantage over us when we apply for academic jobs. We would like to do that too. What do you think?'

"Ben paused, thought about it for a moment, and then said to me, 'Unlike Stanley's students, my students will wait until they have something to say before publishing!' Although this was not the response that my fellow students and I had hoped to hear, we were no longer in doubt about Ben's view on the subject."

Chapter 23

Not Every Effort Is a Success

George Engelhard, Jr.

Writing for publication is a frustrating experience. Prospective authors often spend countless hours laboring over a manuscript that describes a new theory or research study. They then send the fruits of their hard work to a journal editor in hopes that the scholars selected to review the manuscript will recognize its value and the significance of its contribution to the field. But more often than not, a letter or email message from the editor arrives several months later with scathing comments from reviewers. In some cases the reviewers question not only the significance of the work, but the authors' judgment in devoting so much time and energy to what they consider to be a trifling endeavor. Experiences such as these challenge the confidence of even the most self-assured writers and researchers.

George Engelhard, Jr., a professor of education at Emory University and former student of Ben's, had just such an experience while still a graduate student at the University of Chicago. A manuscript on which George had worked for several months was returned from an editor with particularly harsh comments. The reviewers had found little of value in the manuscript and offered no hope that any revision would prove worthy of publication. George shared the following story describing Ben's reaction:

"Feeling both embarrassed and disheartened, I described to Ben what had happened, hoping for sympathy and consolation. But much to his surprise, he offered neither. In fact, he seemed to regard my story as rather matter-of-fact and saw no reason for my anguish or disappointment. Perplexed by his reaction, I questioned him further, again hoping for a more supportive response. Ben rose from his desk and said, 'Follow me.'

George Engelhard, Jr.

"He then led me to a large cabinet in his office and opened the door, pointing to a stack of papers piled nearly three feet high on the cabinet floor. 'What's that?' I asked.

"'They're my rejections,' he answered, 'articles and funding proposals mostly. The majority eventually got published or funded. But many required four, five, or six iterations before they were accepted. Others have never made it beyond this closet.'

"I was dumbfounded. I had always assumed that the quality of Ben's research and writing were so superb that editors begged for his articles and that foundations waited in line to fund his research. By showing me this huge stack of unsuccessful articles and proposals, he helped me see that he, too, had received his share of rejections.

"As he closed the cabinet door, Ben explained to me that few people know about all the failures. Only successes are listed on curriculum vitae. But for every line describing a success, there are untold numbers of setbacks and failures. The key to a successful career, he stressed, is what you do after the failures. Being persistent and maintaining a strong belief in the value of one's work are the marks of a truly successful scholar.

"Ben's frankness and willingness to share his failures had a profound effect on me and on my attitude toward the inevitable setbacks in every scholar's career. So today, when one of those scathing reviews arrives, I always think back to that stack of papers in the bottom of Ben's closet, and immediately begin planning the revision."

Chapter 24

Compensatory Education for Cultural Deprivation

Thomas R. Guskey

The 1960s marked a time of great change in education in the United States, particularly in terms of the federal government's role. The framers of the U.S. Constitution had considered education one of the "reserved powers" left to individual states. But events during the 1950s convinced many at the national level that the states were remiss in their responsibilities and that the federal government needed to intervene. The successful launch of the Sputnik satellite by the Soviet Union was seen as evidence that American schools were behind, especially in mathematics and science education. In addition, landmark court decisions such as *Brown v. Board of Education* in 1954 called attention to the tremendous inequalities in educational opportunity afforded many American children, especially poor and minority children who lived under conditions that at the time were labeled "cultural deprivation."

It was within this context that Ben and two of his University of Chicago colleagues, Allison Davis and Robert Hess, convened the Research Conference on Education and Cultural Deprivation on June 8–12, 1964. The purpose of the conference was to "review what is already known about the problems of education and cultural deprivation, to make recommendations about what might be done to solve some of these problems, and to suggest the critical problems for further research" (Bloom, Davis, & Hess, 1965, p. iii). The U. S. Office of Education provided funding for the conference, and Holt, Rinehart, and Winston agreed to publish the conference proceedings under the title *Compensatory Education for Cultural Deprivation* (Bloom, Davis, & Hess, 1965).

Ben was keenly aware of the problems associated with cultural deprivation and the critical importance of concerted efforts to address those problems. But to him, these problems related not only to educational issues, but to societal and moral issues as well. With his colleagues, he described these problems in the preface to the conference proceedings:

> Very few problems in the field of education are as complex as the problems of cultural deprivation. An adequate attack on these educational problems requires that educational policy makers, curriculum specialists, teachers, guidance workers, and administrators have an appreciation of the many ways in which the social problems of our society bear directly on the development of the child and adolescent, and influence the interaction between students and the schools. (Bloom, Davis, & Hess, 1965, preface)

The conference report contained a series of recommendations, many of which found their way into public policy. Ironically, most of the issues these recommendations were designed to address remain just as relevant today as they were in the 1960s. The recommendations offered were organized into five sections:

1. Basic needs: For example, every child should be assured of an adequate breakfast to help him or her begin the learning tasks of the day (p. 10).
2. Early experiences: For example, parents must be sufficiently involved in the nursery school and kindergarten experience to understand its importance for their child and to give support and reinforcement to the tasks of these special schools (p. 19).
3. Elementary school: For example, the emphasis in the first three years of elementary school should be on the development of every child with careful evaluation records of his or her progress toward clear-cut tasks and goals. . . . The careful sequential development of each child must be one of continual success at small tasks (p. 25).
4. Special case of the Negro students: For example, especially in the early years of school all children must learn under the most positive set of human interactions. Where possible, teachers should be chosen because of their ability to help young children and because they can be warm and supportive of all children (p. 32).
5. Adolescent education: For example, there should be work-study plans in which students can learn in relation to the work. This requires very effective cooperation between schools, industry, and public agencies (pp. 38–39).

Ben, Allison Davis, and Robert Hess realized full well that not all of the recommendations coming from this conference would be accepted. Nevertheless, they were convinced that the future of the United States as a nation and its stature in the world community was inescapably linked to its efforts to properly educate culturally disadvantaged children. Again, in the preface to *Compensatory Education*, they stressed, "We would urge that groups which take exception to our recommendations provide alternatives which are as carefully conceived as we have tried to make ours. To do nothing is really not an alternative to the recommendations we have made in this report" (preface).

This work, along with Ben's earlier work in developing *Stability and Change in Human Characteristics* (Bloom, 1964), provided a foundation for two major congressional acts passed during the mid-1960s as part of President Lyndon Johnson's "War on Poverty." The first was the Economic Opportunity Act (EOA) of 1964, which established the Head Start program. The second was the Elementary and Secondary Education Act (ESEA) of 1965, which created the Title I and Follow Through programs.

Title I was a massive program designed to provide special resources and financial support to school districts that enrolled large numbers of economically disadvantaged, low-achieving students. The Follow Through program was intended to build upon the Head Start program by extending educational support for disadvantaged students from kindergarten through the third grade. These two programs, in combination with Head Start, were grouped under the label "compensatory education." They represented the federal government's first major attempt to become involved in education reform efforts throughout the United States—an effort that continues to this day.

Although the language has changed, these persistent problems remain the focus of education improvement efforts still today. The phrase "cultural deprivation" has been replaced by "economically disadvantaged" to reflect a problem that is related more to poverty and economic conditions than cultural or ethnic background. Nevertheless, the emphasis on closing "gaps" in student achievement among students from different social and economic backgrounds (Blank, 2011) and the 2001 No Child Left Behind Act requirement that assessment results be disaggregated to show the achievement of different student subgroups based on poverty, language, ethnicity, and disability, all stem from the same concerns that Ben, Allison Davis, and Robert Hess raised nearly fifty years ago.

Chapter 25

A Man of Principle

Neville Postlethwaite

Although his work dealt with some of education's most complex problems, the principles by which Ben conducted his work and led his life were simple and forthright. He was intolerant of prejudice and injustice. He insisted that even the most heated debates stay focused on professional issues and never diminish to personal attacks. He was honest to a fault and intensely loyal. He stuck by his friends and was the first to rise to their defense, especially when a principle was involved.

Neville Postlethwaite, professor emeritus at the University of Hamburg and a colleague of Ben's through their work with the International Association for the Evaluation of Educational Achievement (IEA), witnessed this many times. He offered the following story:

"Ben Bloom was the best example I have ever known of a Talmudic scholar. He had this uncanny ability to take a problem and turn it round and round, rather like a prism, until he saw his way through it. He also had great tenacity and perspicacity when undertaking such a task. To me and to many of those who knew him, observing Ben in this kind of thinking process was a great learning experience in itself.

"Ben further amazed me in his ability to estimate what would be important in education in five and ten years from the present. His view of education was larger and grander than most, and he always had the 'big picture' in mind. The unmistakable driving force behind that 'big picture' was Ben's intense desire to improve education in general for the benefit of all students.

"In 1965, Ben, Torsten Husén, and I traveled together to Moscow to hold discussions with the USSR Academy of Pedagogical Sciences about their possible participation in the IEA studies. We were scheduled to fly from East Berlin to Moscow, but first spent three days in West Berlin at the Hotel Lichtburg, not far from the Kurfurstendam. Torsten had promised to give a speech at the conference of the Comparative Education Society in Europe (CESE), which was meeting in West Berlin, prior to his departure for Moscow.

"While Torsten was away at the conference, Ben and I stayed at the hotel to begin work on a grant proposal for over a million dollars to fund the first phase of the IEA six-subject study, a grant that was eventually funded. When Torsten returned from the conference after the first day, he insisted that Ben and I join him the next day to hear a presentation by American researcher Frank Bowles, who all three of us knew. While welcoming the invitation, I suggested that Torsten make sure we would be welcomed since neither Ben nor I were members of CESE.

"The next morning Torsten telephoned from the conference with the answer that Ben and I could not attend the presentation because we were not CESE members. I was satisfied with the response and saw it as an opportunity for continued work on the proposal.

"As we resumed our writing, however, I noticed Ben becoming increasingly agitated. Finally, unable to contain his anger any longer, he rose from the table where we were working and announced that such a response was totally unacceptable. At the time Ben was president of the American Educational Research Association (AERA), the premier association of educational researchers in North America. As president, he believed that he should be welcomed at a meeting of any other learned society. So he sat down and wrote a rather scathing letter to the president of the CESE pointing this out, and had the letter delivered immediately by courier.

"The next morning the secretary of the CESE arrived at our hotel with an apologetic response, formally inviting Ben to attend the conference. When Ben asked if the invitation included me, he was told that it did not. Ben stared coldly at the secretary. 'Professor Postlethwaite is a respected researcher and professional colleague,' he began. 'We are here together working on a proposal for research in comparative education. Please go back and tell your masters that if Postlethwaite is not welcome, then Bloom is not coming.'

"No further response came, and Ben and I stayed at the hotel to continue our work on the proposal. Oddly, later that afternoon the hotel staff informed us that a mix-up had occurred and only two rooms would be available that night for the three of us. So Ben and I were forced to share a double bed during our last night in West Berlin.

"The next day Ben, Torsten, and I flew to Moscow after having entered East Berlin via Checkpoint Charlie. Our meeting with the leaders of the USSR Academy went well, but led to two surprises. First, we discovered that the Soviet researchers had very limited experience in sample survey research in education. And second, we found that these researchers seemed not to take lunch. Our discussions ran to noon, past 1:00 p.m. and 2:00 p.m., and then on to 3:00 p.m. Finally at 4:00 p.m., having grown quite hungry, we asked if we might take a break for some food. A rather vague reply came through interpreters that if we could hold out just a little longer, all would be well.

"At 5:00 p.m. our entire group was taken in state cars to a Georgian restaurant where the tables were overflowing with the very finest culinary delights. We quickly realized that this was special treatment, indeed. The food at our hotel was indifferent at best and that which we sampled at nearby restaurants was worse. This food, however, was exceptional, and it soon became clear that we were being treated as very high-level dignitaries. The evening was filled with innumerable vodka toasts to all sorts of good causes and ended with hearty hugs. Despite the many promises made and goodwill shared, however, it would be more than twenty years before the USSR joined the IEA effort."

Chapter 26

An Uncompromising
Commitment to Excellence

Bobbie Anthony-Perez

Ben insisted on excellence from all of his students and was stubbornly unwilling to settle for less, regardless of the circumstances. He tended to see requests by students for minor accommodations on his part as a major compromise to his standards. This led many students to regard him as inflexible and unreasonably obstinate. It drove some away and led to crushing disappointments for others. Later, however, nearly all discovered that Ben had only their best interests in mind, and they ended up being thankful for his demanding and uncompromising ways.

Bobbie Anthony-Perez, former emeritus professor of psychology at Chicago State University and former student of Ben's, was one of those who experienced firsthand Ben's inflexibility. This is her story:

"In the spring of 1967 I completed, at long last, a final draft of my doctoral dissertation. I had already gone through several extensive revisions and was confident that this version would meet with Ben's approval. Knowing that he was leaving on a professional trip to Israel that summer, I was particularly anxious to be finished. Plans for my graduation were in place, the date was set, and family members had already begun making travel arrangements to attend the ceremony.

"At the appointed time, I went to Ben's office, fully expecting to receive his approval so that I could take the necessary steps for my graduation in June. When he handed me the three-hundred-page document, however, my anticipation turned to grave disappointment. The cover was filled with notes requesting further revision and nearly every page had additional recommendations for change. Leafing through the marked copy, I realized that I could never complete the work required to graduate in June. And with Ben's anticipated departure for Israel,

I could not expect to graduate until the following autumn or perhaps even the winter quarter.

"Ben, of course, knew of my plans and realized my disappointment. But the dissertation was not what he thought it should be; nor was it as good as he believed it could be. Fighting back the tears, I looked at him for an explanation. He had been watching me the entire time and said simply, 'I'm sorry, Bobbie, but I know you can do better.'

"I left the office with the dissertation clenched in my hand, but made it only as far as the women's restroom at the end of the hallway. I went into one of the stalls, sat down, and cried for nearly an hour.

"When Ben returned from Israel in the autumn, I was waiting with a thoroughly revised dissertation, having spent most of the summer making the changes that he recommended and adding a few of my own. Ben read the new version, gave his approval, and I received my doctorate degree in Rockefeller Chapel on the University of Chicago campus in December 1967. My dissertation was subsequently cited in the works of professors at both the University of Chicago and the University of Illinois, and was used as a model by many students who graduated after me. Years later in a letter supporting my academic promotion, Ben described my dissertation as 'one of the best to come out of the Department of Education at the University of Chicago.'

"In the end, Ben's thoroughness, constructive criticism, and compassion compelled me to complete a better dissertation than I thought I would ever be able to. The disappointment I experienced turned out to be temporary, but the pride that I felt in what was accomplished endured a lifetime."

Chapter 27

Rites of Passage

Thomas R. Guskey

Certain "rites of passage" marked the progress of students in the Measurement, Evaluation, and Statistical Analysis (MESA) Program, and especially those who worked closely with Ben. Some of these were formal and well known. Others were much more subtle. Perhaps the most overt but understated change related to how Ben addressed you, and then to how you would address him.

At the University of Chicago, faculty members addressed each other as Mr. or Ms., rather than as Doctor or Professor. This was a long-standing tradition at the university based on an accepted standard of equality among scholars. Ben and many other Chicago faculty members extended this tradition to their students. Beginning with our initial meeting and continuing throughout my first year of graduate study in the MESA Program, Ben always addressed me as "Mr. Guskey."

After completing the first year in the program, all MESA students took part in a series of comprehensive examinations, the results of which determined whether or not you would be invited to continue in the program. This grueling, two-day affair required students to respond in writing to a series of multipart questions constructed by each program faculty member. For months beforehand we spent innumerable long hours preparing for these examinations, using materials that had been assembled by past MESA students and handed down from one generation to the next, with each class adding new information on the most recent research and developments in the field. The experience was both intellectually challenging and emotionally draining.

Scoring procedures for these examinations involved faculty members reading each student's response to their questions, judging the quality of the response, and then assigning a grade of either "pass" or "fail." Once scored, the faculty met privately to discuss each student's performance on the examinations and eventual fate in the program. Ben, as the program chair, then met with each student individually to discuss the results of these deliberations. While most students passed these comprehensive examinations, some did not. Those individuals were then "counseled" out of the program. Occasionally they would seek acceptance in another program within the department, but more often they left the university entirely.

At the appointed hour after taking the comprehensive examinations, I walked nervously to Ben's office in Judd Hall to receive the results. Because my name happened to be the first alphabetically among my classmates, mine was the first meeting scheduled. I believed that I had done well on some sections of the examinations, but I knew my responses in other sections left a lot of room for improvement. So I approached the office with trepidation, thinking about how I would explain a "fail" grade to my classmates with whom I had worked so hard, and to my family, who doubted the wisdom of my decision to come to Chicago in the first place.

As I approached Ben's office door, my pace slowed and my breathing became deeper. The door was open, and Ben sat inside at his desk reading. I knocked lightly on the open door to get his attention and squeaked out a faint, "Mr. Bloom?"

Ben looked up and offered a quick "Come in." He set down his book, took off his glasses, rose from his chair, and took a step to meet me. Then he extended his hand to me and said, "Congratulations, Tom, you passed your examinations."

I was elated, of course, to hear that I had passed and would be allowed to continue in the program. My smile was immediate. But what surprised me most was that for the first time, he had called me by my first name, "Tom." Clearly I had been elevated to a new status. Through this arduous ordeal, I had in some measure proven myself worthy. Although we still held the faculty in the highest esteem and referred to them as Mr. and Ms. in all conversations, those who succeeded in passing the comprehensive examinations had reached a certain level of stature in the program and in the department. From that point on, we were referred to by our first names.

Another transition took place some years later. Before I actually completed my dissertation and graduated, I left the University of Chicago to take a position as assistant professor at the University of Kentucky. This meant, of course, that much of my time during my first year as a new professor was spent writing and revising my dissertation under Ben's direction. We spoke regularly by phone, and I made several trips to Chicago to meet with him. During these conversations and visits I referred to him, as I always had, as "Mr. Bloom."

After a lot of hard work and numerous revisions, I defended my dissertation and graduated the following year. Because of my ongoing work with the Chicago Public Schools and the City Colleges of Chicago, however, I still returned to Chicago regularly and often met with Ben when I did. On one occasion, while having lunch together at the Quadrangle Club on the University of Chicago campus, I referred to him in our conversation as "Mr. Bloom." Ben put his hand on my arm and said, "Tom, you've graduated and are a professor in your own right. You may call me Ben."

Again, I felt elevated to a new status. I was now part of the professoriate—that distinguished community of scholars—and was no longer a student. We were now, at least by his reckoning, professional colleagues. Although I honestly was never able to regard him as a colleague and peer, I will never forget the profound sense of honor and pride that I felt knowing that he regarded me in that way.

Chapter 28

Sophie's Influence

James H. Block

Although Ben collaborated with many distinguished scholars over the course of his career, his closest and most valued collaborator was always his wife, Sophie. Those who knew him well knew that Ben trusted Sophie's judgment implicitly. But few understood fully what a powerful influence her individual professional endeavors had on his thinking and his writing. James Block, former professor of education at the University of California at Santa Barbara and former student of Ben's, made clear Sophie's influence in the following story:

"During the 1960s and continuing through the 1970s, Sophie Bloom did pioneering work on the effectiveness of tutoring. She described the specific aspects of tutoring that make it such a powerful form of instruction and proposed practical strategies for using both peer and cross-age tutoring in modern classrooms (S. Bloom, 1976). Her ideas on tutoring greatly influenced Ben's work in the development of mastery learning. The notion that one might routinely generate in *all* students the positive effects that good tutors generate in a few was also a recurring theme in his later work on the 'two-sigma problem' and the development of talent. Some saw Ben as the originator of these insightful and instructionally powerful ideas. A close reading of his books and articles shows, however, that he consistently cites Sophie's work as the origin and inspiration for them."

Chapter 29

"Learning for Mastery"

Thomas R. Guskey

Ben's work on *Stability and Change* (Bloom, 1964a) and *Compensatory Education* (Bloom, Davis, & Hess, 1965) showed the powerful influence of environmental factors on individuals' cognitive development. This foundation led him in the late 1960s to turn his attention to how best to take advantage of that influence in schools, particularly through classroom instruction.

Great teachers throughout history, such as Comenius, Pestalozzi, and Herbart, struggled with how to make instruction more appropriate for their students. They believed that if they could somehow adapt their instructional activities to better meet the unique learning needs of individual students, virtually all might learn well and reach a very high level of achievement (Bloom, 1974c). Such results are typical in tutorial situations where an individual teacher works with a single student. The challenge lies in finding efficient and effective ways to attain these same results in group-based instructional settings. This premise formed the basis for Ben's renowned article "Learning for Mastery" (Bloom, 1968a), which established the basis of mastery learning.

Ben described mastery learning in this article as both a theory and set of practices designed to help teachers provide higher quality and more appropriate instruction for students. Under these more favorable learning conditions, he theorized that nearly all students would be able to learn quite well and truly "master" any subject. To Ben, the need for such conditions was obvious:

Most teachers begin a new term (or course) with the expectation that about a third of their students will adequately learn what they have to teach. They expect about a third of their students to fail or just "get by." Finally, they expect another third to learn a good deal of what they have to teach, but not enough to be regarded as "good students." . . . The cost of this system in reducing opportunities for further learning and in alienating youth from both school and society is so great that no society can tolerate it for long. Most students (perhaps over 90 percent) can master what we have to teach them, and it is the task of instruction to find the means that will enable our students to master the subject under consideration. (Bloom, 1968a, p. 1)

JOHN B. CARROLL'S "MODEL FOR SCHOOL LEARNING"

Although Ben traced the roots of his ideas on "Learning for Mastery" to the writings of the early Greeks, a major influence in his thinking was a 1963 article by Harvard University professor John B. Carroll entitled "A Model for School Learning." In this article, Carroll challenged long-held notions about student *aptitude*. He pointed out that aptitude traditionally had been viewed as the *level* to which a child could learn a particular subject. Children with high aptitude would be able to learn the complexities of that subject, while children with low aptitude would be able to learn only the most basic elements. When aptitude is viewed in this way, children are seen as either good learners (high aptitude) or poor learners (low aptitude) with regard to a subject.

Carroll argued, however, that student aptitude more accurately reflects an index of *learning rate*. That is, all children have the potential to learn quite well but differ in terms of the time they require to do so. Some children are able to learn a subject very quickly while others take much longer. When aptitude is viewed as an index of learning rate, children are seen not as good and poor learners, but rather as fast and slow learners.

Carroll's proposed "model for school learning" was based on this alternative view of aptitude. He believed that if each child was allowed the time needed to learn a subject to some criterion level, and if the child spent that time appropriately, then the child would probably attain the specified level of achievement. But if not enough time were allowed or if the child did not spend the time required, then the child would learn much less. Thus the degree of learning attained by a child could be expressed by the following simple equation:

$$\text{Degree of Learning} = f\left(\frac{\text{Time Spent}}{\text{Time Needed}}\right)$$

In other words, the degree of learning is a function of the time a child actually spends on learning, relative to the time he or she needs to spend. If the time spent were equal to the time needed, learning would be complete and the equation would equal 1. However, if the time spent were less than the time needed, learning would be incomplete by that proportion.

Carroll further identified the factors that he believed influenced the time spent and the time needed. He theorized that both of these elements were affected by characteristics of the learner and by characteristics of the instruction. Specifically, the time spent was thought to be determined by a learner's *perseverance* and the *opportunity to learn*. Perseverance is simply the amount of time a child is willing to spend actively engaged in learning. Opportunity to learn is the classroom time allotted to the learning. The time needed, on the other hand, Carroll believed was determined by the child's *learning rate* for that subject, the *quality of the instruction*, and the child's *ability to understand the instruction*. Thus:

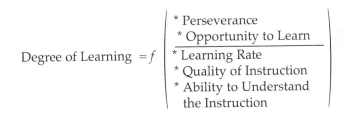

$$\text{Degree of Learning} = f \left(\frac{\text{* Perseverance} \quad \text{* Opportunity to Learn}}{\begin{array}{l}\text{* Learning Rate} \\ \text{* Quality of Instruction} \\ \text{* Ability to Understand} \\ \quad \text{the Instruction}\end{array}} \right)$$

Again, a child's learning rate is a measure of the time required by the child to learn the concepts and skills under ideal instructional conditions. If the quality of the instruction was very high, then the child would readily understand it and would probably need little time to learn. But if the quality of the instruction was not as high, then the child would have greater difficulty understanding and would require much more time in order to learn.

Carroll's article was a significant contribution to learning theory. It set forth new guidelines for research into the concept of aptitude and identified specific factors that influence learning in school settings. His ideas about learning rate also prompted the development of a multitude of new "individualized instruction" programs that allowed students to progress through a series of learning units at their own, self-determined pace. Two of the most popular of these "continuous progress" programs were *Individually Prescribed Instruction* (IPI), developed at the University of Pittsburgh (Glaser, 1966; Scanlon, 1966), and *Individually Guided Education* (IGE), developed at the University of Wisconsin (Klausmeier, 1971; Klausmeier, et al., 1968). Carroll himself, however, did not address the problem of how to provide sufficient time or how to improve instructional quality. These issues were left unresolved.

BLOOM'S "LEARNING FOR MASTERY"

Ben was impressed by the optimism of Carroll's model and particularly by the idea that students differ in terms of the *time required* for complete learning rather than their *ability to learn*. If aptitude was indeed predictive of the time a child required to learn, he believed it should be possible to set the degree of learning expected of each child at some mastery performance level. Then by attending to the instructional variables under the teacher's control—namely the opportunity to learn and the quality of the instruction—the teacher should be able to ensure that each child attain that specified level. In other words, with sufficient time and appropriate instruction, virtually *all students could learn well*.

Ben observed that in most traditional classroom settings, all students are provided with the same opportunity to learn and the same quality of instruction. Those students for whom this time and instruction are appropriate typically learn quite well and master the concepts or learning goals. Those for whom this time and instruction are less appropriate generally learn less well. If, however, the instructional situation could be altered to provide more appropriate opportunities to learn and a more appropriate quality of instruction for each student, then the majority of students, perhaps as many as 90 percent or more, might be expected to learn well and attain mastery.

To determine how this might be practically achieved, Ben drew upon two sources of information. The first was knowledge of the ideal teaching and learning situation in which an excellent tutor is paired with an individual student. He also considered the work of early pioneers in individualized instruction, especially Washburne (1922) and his Winnetka Plan, and Morrison (1926) and his University of Chicago Laboratory School experiments. In considering this work, Ben tried to determine what critical elements of one-to-one tutoring and individualized instruction might be transferred to group-based instructional contexts. The second source from which he drew was descriptions of the learning strategies employed by academically successful students, most particularly the work of Dollard and Miller (1950). Here Ben sought to identify the activities of high-achieving students in group-based learning environments that distinguish them from their less successful classmates.

Ben believed that teachers generally do their best to teach effectively. He found, however, that the quizzes and assessments most teachers use at the end of instructional units do little more than show for whom their instruction was or was not appropriate. If, on the other hand, teachers' quizzes and assessments were accompanied by a *feedback and corrective* procedure, they could serve as valuable learning tools. Specifically, they could be used to *diagnose* individual learning difficulties (feedback) and to *prescribe* specific remediation procedures (correctives).

This type of feedback and corrective procedure is precisely what takes place when an individual student works with an excellent tutor. If the student makes an error, the tutor first points out the error (feedback), and then follows up with further explanation and clarification (corrective). Similarly, academically successful students typically follow up the mistakes they make on quizzes and assessments, seeking further information and greater understanding so that their errors are not repeated.

With this in mind, Ben outlined an instructional strategy to make use of this feedback and corrective procedure. He suggested that the concepts and learning goals students are expected to learn first be organized into instructional units that involve about a week or two of instructional time. Following initial instruction on the unit, a quiz or assessment is administered to students. But instead of signifying the end of the unit, this assessment is used as part of the learning process to give students information, or feedback, on their learning. To emphasize its new purpose, Ben suggested it be called a *formative assessment*—a check on learning used to identify for students precisely what they learned well to that point, and what they need to learn better.

With the formative assessment Ben recommended including specific suggestions to students on what they might do to correct any identified learning difficulties. These corrective activities might point out additional sources of information, identify alternative learning resources, or simply suggest sources of additional practice. The feedback and corrective information gained from a formative assessment provide each student with a detailed prescription of what more needs to be done to master the concepts or desired learning goals from the unit.

Following their corrective work, Ben recommended administering a *second formative assessment*. He stressed that this second assessment should be *parallel* to the first assessment, covering the same concepts and learning goals, but not identical. It was used to verify whether or not the correctives were successful in helping students overcome their individual learning difficulties and to offer students a second chance at success.

Ben also recognized, of course, that some students will do well on the first assessment, demonstrating that they learned the concepts in the unit very well. To ensure the continued learning progress of these students, he recommended providing special *enrichment* or *extension activities* that offer opportunities for these students to broaden and enhance their learning experiences.

Through this process of formative assessment, combined with the systematic correction of individual learning difficulties, Ben believed all students could be provided with a more appropriate quality of instruc-

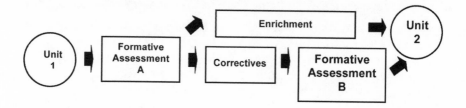

tion than is possible under more traditional approaches to teaching. By providing students with these more favorable learning conditions, he theorized that nearly *all* could learn excellently and truly master the unit concepts and learning goals (Bloom, 1971a, 1976).

THE MASTERY LEARNING PROCESS

Over the years the popularity of mastery learning has grown steadily, and teachers today use it at all levels of education in schools throughout the world. Major programs have been implemented in school districts throughout the United States (S. Anderson, 1994a; Benjamin, 1981; Fiske, 1980; Vickery, 1987), as well as in Asia (Hau-sut, 1990; Kim, et al., 1969, 1970; Wu, 1994), Australia (Chan, 1981), Europe (Dyke, 1988; Langeheine, 1992; Meva-rech, 1985, 1986; Reezigt & Weide, 1990, 1992), and South America (Cabezon, 1984). While some of these programs are relatively small in scale, others have been expanded to include hundreds of teachers and thousands of students.

In addition to its broad application, the effectiveness of mastery learning has been investigated more thoroughly than perhaps any other instructional strategy. Major syntheses of this research have been conducted by Block and Burns (1976), Burns (1986), Guskey and Gates (1986), Guskey and Pigott (1988), Kulik, Kulik, and Bangert-Drowns (1990), Ellis and Fouts (1993), and S. Anderson (1994b). Although these syntheses were done at different times, employed somewhat different selection criteria in choosing the studies to review, and, in some cases, used different review methodologies, all concluded that mastery learning consistently yields exceptionally positive effects on student achievement. In summarizing the results of their extensive meta-analysis, for example, Kulik, Kulik, and Bangert-Drowns (1990) conclude:

We recently reviewed meta-analyses in nearly 40 different areas of educational research (J. Kulik & Kulik, 1989). Few educational treatments of any sort were consistently associated with achievement effects as large as those produced by mastery learning. . . . In evaluation after evaluation, mastery programs have produced impressive gains. (p. 292)

Similarly, in *Research on Educational Innovations*, Ellis and Fouts (1993) conclude that "the research on mastery learning is about as strong as one can find in the annals of educational investigation. Study after study indicates the superiority of mastery learning over traditional methods of instruction" (p. 112).

Ben's ideas on mastery learning profoundly influenced educators in all parts of the world, helping them to provide higher quality instruction for more of their students. In fact, mastery learning is regularly identified as one of the most effective instructional strategies teachers can employ at any level of education (Walberg, 1984). Some researchers have even suggested that the superiority of Japanese students in international comparisons of achievement in mathematics operations and problem solving may be due largely to the widespread use in Japan of instructional practices similar to mastery learning (Waddington, 1995; see also chapter 38 in this book by Akio Nakajima). Even today, mastery learning strategies continue to provide the foundation for many education improvement programs (Guskey, 2009a, 2009b, 2010).

Through mastery learning, Ben extended his theory on the power of educators to help all students learn well. More importantly, he showed how this might be accomplished practically, efficiently, and very effectively.

Chapter 30

Audacity of Imagination

Torsten Husén

Torsten Husén, the eminent educational researcher from Sweden and one of Ben's closest professional friends, related the following story (translated by Kristina Stroede) to illustrate the manner in which Ben's mind worked and his unique way of thinking:

"During the early 1970s, I had the opportunity to visit the United States and had scheduled a meeting with Lee Cronbach, a professor of education at the University of Illinois at the time. Lee and I were discussing current developments in education when the subject of Ben's new work on mastery learning came up. Lee and Ben had been classmates at the University of Chicago, both working under the direction of Ralph Tyler, and they had followed each other's work closely over the years. At one point in our conversation, Lee remarked, 'You must understand, Torsten, Ben likes theories more than facts.' At first I thought the comment seemed condescending and even a bit impolite. But on further reflection, I recognized that Lee was referring to something essential in Ben both as a researcher and as an educational thinker.

"On numerous occasions during our many years of collaboration, I found myself taken aback by the startling observations Ben would make and astonishing conclusions he would reach, many of which seemed well beyond what current research could substantiate. His thinking always seemed to leap ahead of the supporting evidence. But that was simply Ben's style as a researcher. When he put forth a new theory or presented a new interpretation, Ben never limited his ideas to what currently available facts could support. Instead, he put forth daring theories, many of which ran counter to conventional educational wisdom and to what many believed to be sound empirical data. Only later did he set to the task of finding evidence to support his theories. Perhaps the best illustration of this is Ben's theory of mastery learning, in which he asserted that the majority of students, perhaps 90–95 percent, could acquire high levels knowledge and skill—as long as instruction was adapted to meet students' learning needs and sufficient time was provided.

"Ben first shared his ideas about mastery learning with me in 1967 when we were both in London to conduct a press conference for the first large international mathematics study. After an intensive day we took a walk in the area around Piccadilly and stopped in Lyon's Cornerhouse for tea. I was very tired from the events of the day, but when our conversation turned to current research interests, Ben developed newfound energy and became highly animated. He began talking about the studies in which he and his doctoral students were engaged regarding individual differences in school achievement and methods to reduce these differences. The tablecloth became increasingly covered with notes and diagrams as Ben excitedly described these new investigations.

"Ben explained to me the work of Harvard psychologist John B. Carroll, who suggested that the most important factor behind differences in school achievement was not some abstract concept of aptitude, but the *time* an individual needed to learn something. According to Carroll, achievement differences were erroneously attributed to differences in a sort of 'school intelligence,' but they are largely due to individual variation in the need for time. Because the tests and other assessments given in school generally have time limits, they increase differences among students and yield results that are normally distributed. Ben pointed out, however, that there were lots of examples of students learning well when they enjoyed the advantage of high-quality instruction and were given more time. This had always been the case with children who grow up in privileged environments. If educators could be given practical ways to provide high-quality instruction and adequate time for all students, Ben was convinced that *all* could learn to a high standard.

"The idea certainly challenged conventional wisdom. Basically what Ben described to me that night in London was that variation in students' achievement was largely due to school instruction, and that by altering instructional quality and providing sufficient time, such variation could be significantly reduced. As Ben put it, 'Most students become very similar with regard to learning ability, rate of learning, and motivation for further learning—when provided with these favorable learning conditions.' I must confess that I was stunned by Ben's remarkable theory. But I must also admit that I never thought of differences in students' achievement in the same way again.

"Famed American educator John Dewey once remarked, 'Every great advance in science has issued from a new audacity of imagination.' To me, Ben's way of thinking, perhaps more so than any other modern educator, clearly exemplified that kind of audacity of imagination."

Chapter 31

An Appreciation of Arguments

Edward Kifer

Ben held strong beliefs about education and argued passionately in defense of his ideas. But even in the midst of an argument, he never lost his focus or his ability to listen. He always did his best to understand the other person's assumptions and the thinking behind those assumptions for nonjudgmental examination. When disagreements arose, he respected the other person's point of view and typically asked for further elaboration. And even in those instances when he did not win them over, they always parted with a deeper understanding of each other's perspectives.

Edward (Skip) Kifer, former professor of education at the University of Kentucky and former student of Ben's, experienced this firsthand. He offered the following story:

"While working on the International Association for the Evaluation of Educational Achievement's (IEA) Second International Mathematics Study in the mid-1970s, my wife, Suzi, and I were dining with Ben and his wife, Sophie, in Paris. We had a wonderful meal together and shared many stories. At the time, Ben was deeply involved in his work on mastery learning.

"At one point during their dinner, Suzi began questioning Ben about some of his ideas regarding mastery learning. Sitting across the table, I overheard their discussion getting more pointed, with Suzi being critical of certain aspects of Ben's theory. They returned to their conversation throughout the meal, and there seemed to be substantial disagreement between the two parties on many aspects of mastery learning.

"As an assistant professor at the time, I knew that a letter of support from Benjamin Bloom for my promotion and tenure would be, to say the least, invaluable. Being concerned about my future in academia, I was deeply worried that Suzi's attack on mastery learning might influence the support I would need.

"I need not have worried, however. As we were leaving the restaurant, Ben turned to me and said, 'I just had the most pleasant and fascinating conversation with Suzi!' It was clear he had thoroughly enjoyed their talk and, pointed as it was, came away impressed by the thoughtfulness of her comments. Later I received a strong and exceptionally laudatory letter of support from Ben for my academic promotion."

Chapter 32

In His Own Words

Peter Airasian and Thomas R. Guskey

Ben was a constant and fastidious writer. He was convinced that writing brought clarity to thought, and continually reminded his students of the fact. When approached by a student to discuss an idea for a research project or doctoral dissertation, Ben's response was always, "Write two pages on your idea for me, and then we'll discuss what you've written." He shared with me that this modest request typically delayed the discussion for several weeks, but always made it much more productive.

In his own writing Ben chose his words carefully. He believed that when ideas were misinterpreted or misunderstood, it was usually the fault of the writer. To avoid such dilemmas, he often spent hours laboring over a sentence or paragraph to ensure precision in his meaning. "Teaching is a vital part of our work," he often remarked, "but writing is how we communicate ideas to the world and advance the field of education."

Ironically, writing is also the only area in which I ever heard him fault Ralph Tyler. It was not the quality of Tyler's writing that he faulted, of course. Ben frequently remarked that Tyler wrote with amazing clarity and served as his personal model for lucidity. Rather it was the frequency. "Ralph just didn't write enough," Ben said, "and as a result, many of his wonderful ideas and insights were known only by those with whom he spoke."

The most critical and most trusted reviewer of Ben's writing was his wife, Sophie, who read every version of nearly everything that he wrote. Ben trusted her judgment unequivocally. He once told me that he discovered the best way to judge the clarity of his writing was to study Sophie as she read it. "If I see her stop to reread a paragraph or section," he explained, "I know that's something I must revise."

Frequently Ben also asked his students to read the articles or book chapters on which he was working. It was never clear, however, whether this was for his benefit or for the benefit of his students. Certainly it helped us to understand better the problems on which he was working at the time and his thinking with regard to those problems. But while he always asked for our opinions and suggestions for improvement, only rarely did these recommendations result in significant change. Peter Airasian, former professor of education at Boston College and a former student of Ben's, offered a telling example of this:

"In 1968 Ben was asked to write a chapter, 'A Theory of Testing Which Includes Measurement-Evaluation-Assessment,' for a book edited by Merlin C. Witrock and David E. Wiley entitled *The Evaluation of Instruction*. I knew that he was working on the chapter and occasionally inquired as to how it was going. One afternoon Ben appeared in the office where I was working in Judd Hall, gave me a draft of the chapter, and asked me to meet with him a week later to discuss it. As I read the draft, however, I became more and more nervous. To my mind, Ben had not come close to the promised title of an integrated theory of measurement, evaluation, and assessment.

"On the appointed day, I met Ben in his office where I suggested, ever so cautiously, that the integration of the three forms did not quite coalesce and that perhaps more focus could be addressed to the integration of the three approaches. After a thirty-minute discussion that felt to me more like two hours, Ben thanked me very much for my comments and suggestions, and added that they were both thoughtful and helpful. I left the meeting feeling quite proud of myself that day.

"Nearly two years later the book finally appeared, and I rushed to see how my suggestions had been incorporated in the chapter. Ben had indeed made changes, but none were those that I had suggested. In fact, the only change that I could find in the chapter coming from my ideas was that Ben had changed the original title from 'A Theory of Testing Which Includes Measurement-Evaluation-Assessment' to '*Toward* a Theory of Testing Which Includes Measurement-Evaluation-Assessment' (Bloom, 1970). Apparently Ben believed that his original words were quite adequate."

I had a similar experience with Ben many years later. During the early 1980s I set out to develop a book on the practical application of Ben's theory of mastery learning. Other students of Ben's, particularly James Block, then professor of education at the University of California at Santa Barbara, and Lorin Anderson, who at that time was professor of education at the University of South Carolina, had provided operational definitions of mastery learning a decade earlier (Block, 1971, 1974; Block & Anderson, 1975). But much had been learned about the process since then and a book presenting these new insights seemed important.

As I neared completion of the book, I called Ben to ask if he would consider writing the foreword. He readily agreed, and I immediately sent the manuscript to him. Within a few weeks his insightful and highly complimentary foreword arrived in the mail. I included it with the manuscript and proudly sent it off to the publisher.

A couple of months later the edited version of the manuscript was returned to me, along with a few minor suggestions for revision in the foreword. I dutifully sent the suggestions to Ben for his consideration. On the day they arrived in his office he phoned me immediately. As soon as I answered, I could tell that he wasn't pleased. "Tom," he said, "I received your editor's comments on my foreword."

Sensing his displeasure I responded rather lightheartedly, "I'm glad to hear that, Ben. So, what do you think?"

"I think you have a choice here. Do you want my words or the editor's?" he answered.

"Well, yours, of course," I replied.

"Then you need to let your editor know that," he said.

And so I did.

Today, *Implementing Mastery Learning* (Guskey, 1985, 1997) is in its second edition and includes Ben's foreword, word for word, just as he wrote it.

Chapter 33

Honored in One's Homeland

James H. Block

Every professor knows how rare it is to be honored by your own institution. Despite the awards that you might gather from professional organizations or other institutions based on the significance of your work, seldom is that contribution recognized at home. For this reason, Ben's appointment as the Charles H. Swift Distinguished Service Professor at the University of Chicago was particularly noteworthy.

James Block, a former professor of education at the University of California at Santa Barbara and former student of Ben's, was in Ben's office in the spring of 1969 when he received notification of his appointment. Jim related the following story of what happened on that day:

"Ben and I were meeting in his office in Judd Hall to discuss several projects based on Ben's recently published article, 'Learning for Mastery' (Bloom, 1968a) when a young messenger appeared at the office door with a small envelope. Ben took the envelope, opened it, and read the letter as I watched. Immediately I knew that it was something big, because Ben pushed back from his desk, lit one of his omnipresent cigarillos, and glowed. Without saying a word, he handed the letter to me. I read it and immediately offered my congratulations. At that point Ben abruptly ended our meeting saying, 'We'll meet another day. It's time for me to go home.' This was news that Ben first wanted to share with his family.

"Having been both an undergraduate and a graduate student at the University of Chicago, I knew what an honor it was to be named a Distinguished Service Professor. The Charles H. Swift Distinguished Service Professorship was previously held by Enrico Fermi, the famed physicist who won the 1938 Nobel Prize in physics and produced the

93

first nuclear chain reaction in 1942. I also knew how stingy the university had been in awarding such professorships to the Department of Education. So I easily understood Ben's pride at that moment. The academic institution to which Ben had devoted his professional life had recognized his contribution to be on par with that of Nobel laureates. It was a proud day, indeed."

Chapter 34

A Grand Vision

Neville Postlethwaite

In the latter part of 1969, Ben suggested to Neville Postlethwaite that the International Association for the Evaluation of Educational Achievement (IEA) should run a six-week seminar on curriculum development for educational leaders from around the world. Neville was initially cool to the idea, believing that IEA was in the business of conducting research, not in running seminars. But Ben, seeing this as an essential building block for the IEA's ambitious work, pressed for the idea with great enthusiasm and finally won over Neville, who offered the following story of their work together at that time:

"Together Ben and I approached Torsten Husén, then chairman of IEA, and shared the idea of the seminar with him. Like me, Torsten's initial response was one of skepticism. He saw such an endeavor as a lot of additional work for IEA at a time when the organization was already bogged down with its own elaborate research agenda. But he agreed to let Ben and me attempt to find funding for the seminar, thinking that would temper Ben's enthusiasm and perhaps put an end to the idea.

"Getting the first foundation to see the value of such a worldwide event was difficult. But after the first was on board, others followed, and Ben and I soon had all the funding we needed. Based on past experiences, Ben was concerned that the invited countries would not send their best and brightest curriculum specialists to such an extended seminar. So he insisted on going round the world to visit the various ministries of education in order to set down the criteria to be used within each ministry for selecting candidates. When not visiting the different countries, Ben was busy convincing some of the best curriculum minds in the world to serve as faculty members for the seminar.

"In the summer of 1971, the seminar was held in Gränna, Sweden. It included teams of six curriculum specialists from each of twenty-three countries. The faculty was a star-studded cast of academics and curriculum specialists from around the world, the senior one of whom was Ralph W. Tyler. Ralph spent the entire six weeks at the seminar, and it is said that it was the first time in years that he had stayed so long in one place.

"What came to be known as the 'Gränna seminar' turned out to be a great success with its effects seen in ministries of education throughout the world for decades afterward. Never before, and never since, has such a grand event of worldwide cooperation in education occurred. Ben realized his grand vision by refusing to be put off by the myriad difficulties and setbacks that would have squelched the enthusiasm of lesser men. Through persistence, dedication, and hard work, his hope became a reality of profound significance."

Chapter 35

Collaborative Leadership

John Goodlad

John I. Goodlad, emeritus professor of education at the University of Washington, became a professional colleague of Ben's when he returned to the University of Chicago in 1956. Although John had been a graduate student at Chicago in the late 1940s, he had few interactions with Ben, who was then a young assistant professor. Upon reflecting on Ben and his contributions, John offered the following story:

"After graduating from the University of Chicago, I took a faculty position at Emory University. It was during that time that Ben sent me an early draft of what was to become the *Taxonomy of Educational Objectives, Handbook 1: The Cognitive Domain* (Bloom, et al., 1956), asking for my reactions. I went through the manuscript and passed it along to others. While most were greatly impressed and praised it as a contribution of immense significance, a few saw it as a frightening instance of reductionism in education that dehumanized the processes of human learning and thinking. The group of university examiners that Ben directed in developing the *Taxonomy* had anticipated this reaction, of course, but it still became a major criticism of *Taxonomy* after the volume was published.

"Just as John Dewey had found it necessary to counter the excesses of disciples in their interpretation of his work, I believe that Ben also found it necessary to reject the mechanistic applications of *Taxonomy* that ensued after its publication. He intended the work to draw attention to the low cognitive levels so commonly stressed in the pedagogy of schooling and especially emphasized in most educational testing. Indeed, when Ben was invited to India as a consultant because of concern among educators there that testing was too rigid and played too critical a role in the lives of aspiring students, he surprised his hosts in recommending not the elimination of testing as anticipated, but the introduction of more comprehensive assessments of students' application and analysis skills, along with other higher mental processes.

"Unfortunately, the frequent price of work that gains widespread recognition is that of obscuring other contributions in a creative career. This is what I believe happened to some degree to Ben. The popularity and acceptance of *Taxonomy* as a framework for the development of curricula detracted from the importance of Ben's book, *Stability and Change in Human Characteristics* (Bloom, 1964), which so powerfully influenced the field of early childhood education. In some ways it also overshadowed what I believe to be Ben's most significant contribution: his work in establishing the International Association for the Evaluation of Educational Achievement (IEA).

"In the 1960s and 1970s, the work done in most countries' national curriculum centers tended to range from chaotic to rigidly bureaucratic. Where the work was most systematic, it also tended to be highly political and largely divorced from scholarly inquiry. Based on his experiences with the curriculum center in India, for which he served as a consultant and critical friend, Ben saw the possibilities for correcting this situation and improving the curricular and evaluative processes of schooling on an international scale. So he turned his enormous energies and keen intellect to developing a model of international cooperation in curriculum development and evaluation. His vision led to the establishment of new national centers of curriculum and evaluation in countries throughout the world, coordinated through a headquarters in Sweden. These centers worked to make curriculum development a thoughtful and scholarly process rather than a political exercise.

"Ben's dream came together in the summer of 1971 with the six-week international gathering that took place in Gränna, Sweden. An event of this magnitude was unprecedented in the field of education. In addition, it took place at the height of the Vietnam War, when international cooperation in any endeavor was extremely rare. But thanks to Ben's leadership, the financial assistance of several international organizations, and the creativity and hard work of such people as Torsten Husén, Neville Postlethwaite, Ralph Tyler, and others, teams of six people each from twenty-three countries assembled at a conference center located on one of Sweden's most picturesque lakes. Their assignment was to learn more about curriculum, evaluation, and innovation in education and to plan the future of national curriculum centers in their diverse homelands. Only a couple of the invited countries failed to attend and to send a team of delegates.

"Such a gathering, of course, could have been a recipe for disaster. Much has been written about the stress of individuals leaving their homes and habits to associate closely with strangers, while being immersed deeply in complex work involving provocative ideas. Serving as a member of the conference staff, I recall the disbelief and skepticism of many delegations' members. During the first week of the conference, it was clear that several delegation leaders were convinced that they had little if anything in common with the representatives of other countries.

"The difficult task of ensuring collaboration and mutual respect fell mainly to Ben and Sophie Bloom. Had they not taken on the role of 'father and mother' to the entire group, I am convinced that many unpleasant incidents might have occurred. Together, Ben and Sophie shepherded the group through the complex work, making certain that a sense of dignity, respect, and consideration accompanied all professional and personal exchanges.

"Ben's keen sense of group dynamics also helped him structure the conference to keep everyone's focus on the tasks at hand. Realizing that visitors rarely understand or fully appreciate how a unique culture develops in such situations and how easy it is for visitors to upset the customs beginning to solidify, for example, Ben made it clear to all sources that visitors were not to be invited. Unfortunately, this did not prevent a few representatives of the sponsoring organizations from appearing for a day or two. These occasions, I believe, were the closest the group came to crisis during the conference. The incredible administrative and organizational skills of Neville Postlethwaite and the other staff members from the center in Sweden helped to keep things running smoothly during these troubled times. Still, it was primarily Ben and Sophie, working behind the scenes, who kept the conference a very civil enterprise of unparalleled sharing and professional collaboration.

"Ben was ever present throughout the conference. He calmly and humorously welcomed the total group for the plenary sessions each morning, pulled the staff together quickly whenever an issue or problem had any potential for getting out of hand, introduced speakers and special resource people in such a way that their contributions fit into the complex mosaic of the ongoing work, drifted quietly into the smaller group meetings that occurred each afternoon, and never missed any of the specially arranged functions.

"During those weeks Ben also talked extensively with conference staff members, many of whom were former or present students of Ben's, about possible next steps for this international network of national curriculum and evaluation centers. They discussed potential funding sources, the role of the planned headquarters in Paris, an advisory body, and the executive officers.

"At the end of the six weeks, with the different accents still ringing in their ears and plans for continued work in their hands, the conference participants dispersed. Strangers just a few weeks earlier, they shared hugs and tearful goodbyes as dear friends in the airport hubs of Amsterdam and London.

"During the following year, Ben assembled a small group of those who had been part of the Gränna conference in Paris for further conversations. Ben and Torsten Husén were both cautiously optimistic about the prospect for programmatic funds but less than encouraged in their efforts to secure funds for the necessary secretariat in Paris. Ben spoke of his plans for an impending trip to countries that had been represented in Gränna in order to test the waters of interest in each. Some of the conference staff also spoke of individual invitations to visit the home countries of those with whom they had been most closely associated during the conference.

"Hopes for sustained collaboration continued for several years. But advancing instability in the world's economy made it exceedingly difficult to obtain the funds necessary for such a robust, worldwide educational venture. While collaborative efforts were maintained among many of the participating countries, especially regarding the collection and evaluation of data for international comparisons of educational attainment, it was not nearly of the scope and breadth that Ben had originally envisioned.

"Eventually the hopes of Ben and most of the others who had worked with such passion and energy to build an international alliance of curriculum and evaluation centers began to fade. Political and economic problems were greater than anticipated and in many cases proved to be insurmountable. Although Ben never made mention of it publicly, I believe this may have been Ben's greatest professional disappointment. In retrospect, however, it was a monumental achievement. Never before in the history of education throughout the world had anything so grand ever been attempted. In addition, the collaborative exchange initiated through this effort provided the basis for numerous international cooperative programs from that time forward. The success of international comparisons of educational achievement today is owed largely to the vision of Benjamin Bloom over four decades ago."

Chapter 36

Human Characteristics
and School Learning

Thomas R. Guskey

The late 1960s and early 1970s were a time of great pessimism in education. The much-touted report on *Equality of Educational Opportunity* (Coleman, et al., 1966) indicated that schools did little to help students learn, particularly minority children. Instead, this report contended that students' achievement in school was determined primarily by social, demographic, and economic factors that lie beyond the control of educators. As a result, it became popular in the late 1960s to criticize teachers and schools, and there appeared to be growing uneasiness about supporting educational endeavors with public funds (Good, 1983).

It was in this context that Ben put forth his most powerful and perhaps most controversial statement about the influence of educators on student learning in his book *Human Characteristics and School Learning* (Bloom, 1976). He had presented the basic theme of the book years earlier in his classic article, "Innocence in Education" (Bloom, 1972), in which he challenged those who doubted educators' potential to help *all* students learn well:

> [For many years] we assumed that most of the causes of success or failure in school learning lay outside the school's or the teacher's responsibility. In our innocence, we were content to talk about *equality of opportunity*, by which we thought of each student being given the same learning conditions—it was the students who differed in their use of this opportunity.
>
> More recently, we have come to understand that under appropriate learning conditions, students differ in the *rate* at which they can learn—not in the *level* to which they can achieve or in their basic capacity to learn. . . . That is, there is growing evidence that much of what we termed *individual differences in school learning* is the effect of particular school conditions rather than of basic differences in the capabilities of our students. (Bloom, 1972, 334–335)

Ben emphasized the same theme in the preface to *Human Characteristics*. He stressed that for a long time the prevailing construct in education had been "there are good learners and poor learners." Good learners could learn the more complex and abstract ideas related to a subject, while poor learners could learn only the simplest and most concrete ideas. This was considered a relatively permanent attribute of individuals, and many school systems around the world were organized on the basis of this construct.

He went on to describe how in the early 1960s, a different construct began to emerge, based on the idea that "There are faster learners and slower learners." While educators were not certain whether or not learning rate was a permanent trait of individuals, efforts were made to find ways to give slower learners the help and extra time they needed to attain some criterion level of achievement. With this help and extra time, large portions of slower learners were able to learn equally complex and abstract ideas, apply those ideas to new problems, and retain those ideas equally well. Furthermore, their interests and attitudes toward the school subjects they learned were just as positive as those of the faster learners.

The third construct, the most revolutionary, and the one on which Ben based his book, was that "most students become very similar with regard to learning ability, rate of learning, and motivation for future learning when provided with favorable learning conditions." This construct explicitly challenged the first two constructs, especially the permanence of good-poor learning ability and fast-slow learning characteristics. But more importantly, Ben stressed that this new construct is not a matter of abstract theory or faith. Rather, he contended that it was based on "easily observed evidence readily obtainable in most of the classrooms of the world" (p. x). Ben emphasized this new construct in describing the purpose of his book in its opening paragraph:

> This is a book about a theory of school learning which attempts to explain individual differences in school learning as well as to determine the ways in which such differences may be altered in the interest of the student, the school, and, ultimately, the society. It attempts to test the view that most students can learn what the schools have to teach—if the problem is approached sensitively and systematically. (Bloom, 1976, p. 1)

On the pages that followed, Ben outlined his theory of school learning, positing that much of the variation in student learning outcomes is attributable to three major factors. The first was students' *cognitive entry behaviors* (CEB)—students' previous learning experiences, especially with regard to the prerequisite learning necessary for the current learning task. The second was students' *affective entry characteristics* (AEC)—the extent to which students are or could be motivated to engage in the learning process. And the third was the *quality of instruction* (QI)—the degree to which the instruction is appropriate for students' learning needs. The four elements that made up the quality of instruction were cues, participation, reinforcement, and feedback/correctives.

Ben also described what he believed were the major outcomes of any learning task. These included the *level and type of achievement*, the *rate of learning*, and the *affective characteristics of the learner* in relation to the learning task and to self. When students' entry characteristics and the quality of instruction are favorable, Ben theorized that all the learning outcomes would be at a high or positive level, and there would be little variation in the measures of these outcomes. If there was considerable variation among students in their entry characteristics and in the quality of instruction, however, he believed there would be great variation in learning outcomes.

MAJOR VARIABLES IN BLOOM'S THEORY OF SCHOOL LEARNING

According to Ben's theory, the two aspects of students' histories (CEB and AEC) and the four elements of quality of instruction interact within the context of a learning task. Any course of study was seen as consisting of a series of such learning tasks. When the relationship among these learning tasks is sequential, which is frequently the case in school learning, the cognitive and affective outcomes of earlier tasks become the cognitive entry behaviors and affective entry characteristics for later tasks. Therefore, if teachers could improve the quality of instruction by enhancing its

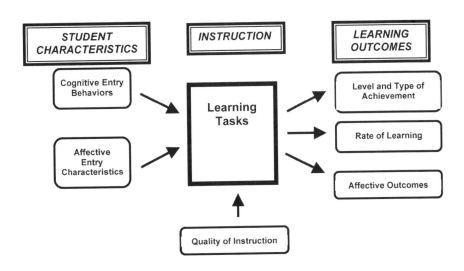

four major elements to ensure that all students "mastered" early learning tasks, then all students would have the necessary prerequisites (CEB and AEC) to do well on subsequent tasks. As a result, all students might attain the same high level of achievement and become more similar in terms of their learning rate, their confidence in future learning situations, and their motivation in subsequent learning tasks. As Ben put it:

> The central thesis of this book is that variations in learning and the level of learning of students are determined by the students' learning history and the quality of instruction they receive. Appropriate modifications related to the history of the learners and the quality of instruction can sharply reduce the variation of students and greatly increase their level of learning and their effectiveness in learning in terms of time and effort expended. Where conditions for learning in the home and school approach some ideal, we believe that individual differences in learning should approach a vanishing point. (Bloom, 1976, p. 16)

Ben emphasized these two basic points throughout the book: (1) that students' abilities to learn a particular set of tasks are highly alterable; and (2) that under ideal conditions the differences among students in terms of their ability to learn, the time and effort they require to learn, the level of achievement they attain, and their motivation for future learning can be greatly reduced. These two points also became a lightning rod for criticism of *Human Characteristics and School Learning*. Some of this criticism came from individuals who disagreed with Ben's assertion about the potentially powerful influence of educators, restating old arguments about the tremendous influence of social, demographic, and economic factors on student achievement. Other criticism came from people who clearly misinterpreted Ben's contention.

Some critics, for example, argued that by suggesting that all students could learn well and reach high levels of achievement, Ben was implying that education should make all students the same. But this was never his contention. Ben recognized that in any instructional situation, some students will learn more than others. In fact, he encouraged teachers to facilitate this by providing students who learn quickly with the opportunity to broaden and extend their learning through specially designed "enrichment activities."

Ben believed, however, that if educators could specify a finite set of learning goals in a curriculum, that is, a specific set of things they want students to learn and be able to do at a predetermined criterion level, then by attending to instructional factors under their control educators could guarantee that all students learned those things excellently. Granted, some students would learn only those things while others would learn that and much more. But in terms of that finite set of learning goals, all students would learn those well. And if all students learn well, then there is little difference among students in terms of their level of achievement. As a result, the differences in students' level of learning *with regard to that specific set of learning goals* would approach a vanishing point (Bloom, 1971a).

Again and again throughout the book, Ben reiterated this same basic idea:

> The main import of the entire book is that human nature is not the barrier to educational and cultural development that philosophers, politicians, social scientists, and educators have frequently alleged. The characteristics of the students and of the instruction dealt with in this book are claimed to be alterable, and *if this is so,* changes in the school environment can relatively quickly (in a single decade) make great changes in the learning of students. In contrast, attempts to make changes in the home and the larger social environment which are believed to be related to education and learning are likely to take many decades before major effects would be felt in the schools. (Bloom, 1976, p. 17)

Oddly, as educators today struggle in their efforts to "close the achievement gap," most neglect the powerful ideas that Ben outlined over a quarter century ago on how this could be accomplished (Guskey, 2005, 2007). But more importantly for Ben, the idea of reducing the variation in students' level of achievement and closing the achievement gap was not simply an educational issue—it was a moral issue. For him, it came down to a basic educational philosophy that was reflected again and again in his work:

> A society which places such great value on education and schooling that it requires the individual to attend school for long periods of time must find the means to make education attractive and meaningful to the individual learner. Modern societies no longer can content themselves with the *selection of talent*; they must find the means for *developing talent.* (Bloom, 1976, p. 17)

Although considered by some to be overly optimistic, *Human Characteristics and School Learning* remains a hallmark work in learning and instructional theory. Since its publication it has been cited over 2,300 times and is referenced in many modern works, including the following titles:

Marzano, R. J., Frontier, T., & Livingston, D. (2011). *Effective supervision: Supporting the art and science of teaching.* Alexandria, VA: Association for Supervision and Curriculum Development.
Novak, J. D. (2010). *Learning, creating, and using knowledge: Concept maps as facilitative tools in schools and corporations* (2nd ed.). New York, NY: Routledge.
Powell, R. G., & Powell, D. L. (2010). *Classroom communication and diversity: Enhancing instructional practice* (2nd ed.). New York, NY: Routledge.

Chapter 37

The Man Who Hated the Normal Curve

Torsten Husén

Although Ben enjoyed longstanding relationships with many international scholars, none was longer than the relationship he shared with Torsten Husén, the eminent educational researcher from Sweden. Torsten had encountered Ben's work long before they met and shared the following story about his experiences (translated by Kristina Stroede):

"During the summer of 1954 I visited Lee Cronbach at the University of Illinois to discuss trends in educational research in the United States. Lee had been a classmate of Ben's at the University of Chicago. During our conversations, Lee shared with me information about a project Ben had initiated to clarify the goals of instruction by establishing a so-called 'taxonomy.' After I returned to Sweden, Lee sent me a draft report from the project. It was entitled 'Taxonomy of Educational Objectives: The Classification of Educational Goals: Cognitive Domain,' and Ben was the main author. The magnitude, insight, and thoughtfulness of this work impressed me greatly. I knew even then that its impact on education would be immense.

"I never actually met Ben until some years later, in the spring of 1960, at the UNESCO Institute for Education in Hamburg, Germany. The institute was an exploratory effort to identify methods for evaluating national educational systems that subsequently led to formation of the International Association for the Evaluation of Educational Achievement, or IEA. Such grand-scale evaluation was a totally new experience for everyone involved in the project. International comparisons would require the development of standardized assessments that included only 'culture-free' items and that could be translated into several different languages. The goal of these assessments was to identify factors that influenced the effects of instruction across various countries and thereby yield a high level of generalization.

"This enormous task required creativity, political savvy, a sense of practicality, and immense technical skill. From my perspective, no one proved more worthy of that ominous task than Ben. His ability to think divergently and his tendency to turn things around and look at them from a variety of different perspectives seemed almost magical to those who worked on the project. It also made Ben a natural leader in many IEA initiatives.

"As the IEA chair, I had numerous opportunities to see Ben in action, often during long meetings in places like Hamburg, Paris, Stockholm, and Chicago. Together Ben, Neville Postlethwaite, and I outlined IEA's Six-Subject Survey project in Moscow, negotiated funding for other international projects in Washington, DC, and organized seminars in Gränna, Sweden, and Paris. The success of these seminars was extraordinary and brought to those involved a true sense of what it meant to be part of 'the international community of scholars.'

"On one particular occasion in 1965, Ben, Neville, and I flew to Moscow together via Schönefeld in East Berlin to negotiate with the Academy of Pedagogical Sciences about the Soviet Union's participation in IEA's mathematics study and possibly the Six-Subject Survey. This was the first time Ben had visited the country from which his father and mother had emigrated in part to escape persecution as Jews. It was also the first time that I got to know Ben not only as an eminent psychologist and educational researcher, but also as a dear friend.

"When IEA first began, project funding was administered by the UNESCO Institute in Hamburg, Germany. But through Ben's efforts, nearly two million dollars of additional funding were secured from the U.S. Office of Education. Because these federal monies could not be awarded to any foreign or international organization, Ben served as principal investigator on these projects and coordinated funding through the University of Chicago. This arrangement required great diplomacy on Ben's part, since the university and IEA officials frequently disagreed on what particular efforts were most worthy of funding.

"In 1970, Ben and I were both in New York City to attend the annual meeting of the American Educational Research Association (AERA). One night the two of us met for dinner to discuss the upcoming IEA seminar that Ben was organizing in Gränna, Sweden. The following day Ben was to receive a prestigious award from AERA and deliver a major presentation.

"During dinner I asked Ben what he planned to say. He hesitated for a moment and then said, 'I will be describing either the beginning of a new era in school research or the end of my own research career.' This was quite a startling statement that took me by surprise. But soon I discovered precisely what Ben meant. In his presentation, he would question the notion that educational outcomes should ever be represented by a normal curve distribution.

"Ben entitled his presentation 'Individual Differences—A Vanishing Point?' Although he posed the title as a question, he knew the ideas he planned to present would challenge most of those in his audience. Some might even consider his ideas foolish because they reached far beyond current knowledge and confirming evidence. Still, Ben was prepared to 'push the envelope,' to be provocative, and to suffer the consequences, whatever those might be.

"Ben's presentation, later published as a *Phi Delta Kappan* monograph (Bloom, 1971a), put forward the premise of his theory on school learning and the foundation of his work on mastery learning. He described how three major factors—cognitive entry behaviors, affective entry characteristics, and the quality of instruction—interact to influence student achievement. By focusing on aspects of these factors that teachers control, Ben hypothesized that it should be possible to decrease the variation in school achievement to close to 10 percent of what is typical. In other words, when provided with favorable learning conditions, most students become very similar with regard to learning ability, rate of learning, and motivation for further learning. Such individual differences would thus reach a vanishing point, and normal curve distributions of student learning outcomes would become a relic of an ineffectual past. If proven valid, Ben's ideas would have far-reaching consequences for teacher education, classroom instruction, the organization of educational systems, methods of grading, and the development of curriculum.

"Above all else, I found that Ben always looked for the best in people and all humankind. In his later years Ben undertook a study that seemed to me to be a natural continuation of his work on mastery learning. He and a small number of his students identified and studied young people who had made absolutely top contributions within areas such as science and mathematics, art and music, and athletics. These individuals, as well as their parents, teachers, and coaches, were interviewed at length to determine what factors in their environment promoted the development of their exceptional talent and brought them to a level of achievement reached by only the smallest minority of people in their field. His idea was that if such factors could be identified, perhaps many more people could be helped to reach these exceptional levels of achievement. I saw this as a reflection of the idea that Ben had presented so many times in his books and articles: 'Modern societies no longer can be content with the *selection* of talent; they must find the means for *developing* talent.'"

Chapter 38

A Powerful Influence
on Japanese Education

Akio Nakajima

Japanese educational leaders were thrilled by the invitation to participate in the International Seminar for Advanced Training in Curriculum and Innovation that Ben had organized in Gränna, Sweden, in 1971. Poised to embark on a major curriculum reform, they saw the seminar as an opportunity to become familiar with the most current research and thinking on curriculum development. Akio Nakajima, who then served as administration officer in the Japanese Ministry of Education and president of the Japan Educational Exchange, shared the following reflection on the experience:

"Four distinguished Japanese educators made up the Japanese delegation to the conference in Gränna, Sweden, two from the Ministry of Education and two from Japan's National Institute for Educational Research. I had the honor of serving as the delegation's leader. Being somewhat familiar with Ben's work in developing the *Taxonomy of Educational Objectives*, I was convinced the seminar could provide the foundation for Japan's new curriculum. I also looked forward to meeting Ben and to working with him personally.

"The long trip to Sweden, accompanied by numerous delays, proved difficult and trying for our delegation. But upon our arrival everyone's spirits were revived when we learned that we would be staying in the same apartment building as Ben and Sophie Bloom. We considered this especially fortunate and hoped it would give us with the opportunity to interact with Ben on a more regular basis during our six weeks in Sweden.

"Despite my limited English language skills, I quickly became an active participant in the seminar and attended as many sessions as possible. I was most impressed by Ben's theories about the *Taxonomy of Educational Objectives* (Bloom, Engelhart, Furst, Hill, & Krathwohl, 1956), the

Handbook on Formative and Summative Evaluation of Student Learning (Bloom, Hastings, & Madaus, 1971), and especially 'Learning for Mastery' (Bloom, 1968a). I was also quite taken by Ben's ideas about establishing a Curriculum Center in each participating country. I envisioned such a center to be a place where educational leaders from throughout Japan would come to develop the needed changes in both the curriculum and instructional practices of Japanese schools.

"One day during the seminar, Ben met in private consultation with our delegation at my request. I used this opportunity to share how impressed the entire delegation was with Ben's theories and, in particular, with his ideas on mastery learning. I then asked Ben if he would recommend to delegation members a set of strategies for implementing mastery learning practices in Japan. Specifically, I wanted Ben's suggestions on how we could use mastery learning in classes that often included more than fifty students and also how we might overcome anticipated resistance from the Japanese teachers' association.

"After listening carefully to our questions and requests, Ben smiled. 'My ideas are purely educational theory,' he said, 'built on hypotheses that we've been able to confirm through relatively small-scale, experimental studies. How to adapt the theory to specific educational systems is *your* task.' He then went on to describe the published work of Dr. Hogwon Kim in Korea, where the educational system was quite similar to Japan's, and offered information on how Dr. Kim could be contacted.

"Initially, Ben's response came as a disappointment to our delegation members. We had hoped to leave Sweden with a detailed plan on how to implement these new ideas. Later we realized, however, that Ben's response was not a put-off, but rather a challenge. Ben shared with us what he believed was possible. It was our job to figure out how to realize that possibility in the schools of Japan. After six weeks our Japanese delegation left Sweden full of new ideas and enthusiasm, and with a profound respect for Ben and his work.

"A year later, in 1972, I along with the other members of the Japanese delegation at the Gränna conference invited Ben to visit Japan and to present a series of lectures on his theories. These were held at the Japanese Ministry of Education, the National Institute of Education, and Tokyo University, and consistently drew very large crowds of educators and researchers. In his lectures Ben described how an increasing number of countries had formed National Curriculum Centers where summative evaluation techniques were used to determine the value of old curricula and ongoing formative evaluations guided the development of new curriculum models. But sadly, his words fell on deaf ears. Despite the efforts of those educational leaders who had been a part of the Gränna conference, the Ministry of Education's Curriculum Council and the National

Diet remained committed to a very traditional curriculum and considered only the most modest level of change.

"It was not until the late 1990s, when the Japanese economy faced its first major recession since the end of the Second World War, that the Central Council for Education recommended the development of a National Curriculum Center, modeled after the ideas Ben set forth twenty-five years earlier. The center opened in January 2001 and began a major effort to revise and modernize the Japanese curriculum in all subject areas.

"Today, I continue in a leadership role in Japanese education reform. I work closely with Dr. Eiichi Kajita, currently the president of the Notre Dame Kyoto Women's University. Since 1974, Dr. Kajita has translated nearly all of Ben's major works into Japanese, making them available to educators at all levels in Japan. As a result, Ben's ideas have helped shape many of the changes taking place in Japanese education. In addition, I initiated a major effort to remodel the Prefectural Education Centers. Traditionally, these regional centers have functioned as only teacher meeting and training facilities. With the current emphasis on decentralizing education in Japan, my hope is that these centers will become places where local teachers, school administrators, and university professors gather to discuss both curriculum and instructional reform, based in large part on Ben's theories from the *Taxonomy of Educational Objectives, Formative and Summative Evaluation of Student Learning,* and 'Learning for Mastery.'"

Chapter 39

High Expectations for All

Judy Eby

Although his kindness was unmatched, Ben was also a harsh taskmaster. He set extraordinarily high expectations for all of his students and accepted no excuses. Meetings in his office to discuss a potential dissertation topic frequently left students feeling that their research ideas were naïve and insignificant, and that their chances of ever graduating were slim at best. On rare occasions, however, such a meeting ended with a smile, a nod, and a challenge to continue exploring a promising idea. Those occasions renewed students' confidence and energy, strengthened their resolve, and kept them going.

Ben was teaching at Northwestern University in 1984 when Judy Eby first met with him to discuss her work on the behavior of "gifted" students. She provided the following story about her experiences in working with Ben:

"At our initial meeting, Mr. Bloom told me that he would be happy to chair my doctoral committee at Northwestern University and to supervise my study, but only if I could work quickly. Having recently retired from his faculty position at the University of Chicago, he had signed only a two-year contract at Northwestern, and was uncertain as to whether he wished to extend that contract. Since I had already decided on the topic for my dissertation and was working full-time on the project, I felt confident that I could complete the work within the time frame that he suggested.

"Things moved along quite well for me until it came time for me to write the first draft of my dissertation. As any good student would do, I went to the Northwestern University library and looked for examples of dissertations on topics similar to mine. Using those dissertations as

112

models, I carefully wrote a draft that I took to Mr. Bloom for his review. When I met with him to discuss the draft, however, he handed me the copy with notes scribbled throughout and said only, 'This is completely unacceptable.'

"Dutifully, I rewrote the draft and submitted it to Mr. Bloom again but, again, received the same response. This went on through several iterations, and each time Mr. Bloom responded with increasing frustration that the work was simply unacceptable.

"One afternoon, following yet another mutually unsatisfying discussion of both the form and substance of my dissertation draft, I left Mr. Bloom's Northwestern office in tears. The disappointment had finally proven too great for me to handle, and I drove home with every intention of dropping out of the Northwestern program.

"Arriving at home, I took a long, hot shower, hoping to regain my composure before sharing the sad news of my decision with my husband. While in the shower, my husband knocked on the bathroom door and said, 'Judy, you have a phone call. It's *Mrs.* Bloom.' I thought he was surely mistaken and meant '*Mr.* Bloom.' But still being too upset to talk, I asked my husband to please take a message.

"About an hour or so later the phone rang again. This time I answered, and a kind voice replied 'Ms. Eby, this is Sophie Bloom. My husband would like to talk to you.'

"After a long moment of silence, Mr. Bloom was on the phone. 'Ms. Eby,' he began, 'my wife thinks I've been too hard on you. Why don't we meet tomorrow in my office at the University of Chicago and see if we can't resolve this problem.' He then gave me directions to his office.

"At the agreed-upon time, I showed up at Mr. Bloom's office in Judd Hall on the University of Chicago campus. There he showed me several dissertations written by his own graduate students from the Measurement, Evaluation, and Statistical Analysis (MESA) Program. With these as models, I again set to the task of rewriting the draft of my dissertation so that both the form and substance met Mr. Bloom's requirements. The effort proved successful, and I successfully completed my degree.

"After my dissertation was accepted, my husband and I asked to meet Mrs. Bloom, the person I believed had played such a key role in the completion of my degree. The four of us went out for dinner together and laughed about the incident that had been such a turning point for me. Since then I have maintained my friendship with Mrs. Bloom, and I consider her to be one of the most influential mentors in my life, as well as Mrs. Bloom's husband, of course."

Chapter 40

Keeping Things in Perspective

Thomas R. Guskey

One of Ben's finest traits was his extraordinary sense of humor. He used this trait well, especially at those times when asked to comment on the significance of his work. His self-effacing nature made it difficult for him to ever take credit for all that he had accomplished. So usually, in a very pleasant and humorous way, he would make light of the compliment.

I recall a conversation we had shortly after the publication of *Human Characteristics and School Learning* (Bloom, 1976). Ben was quite renowned in education circles throughout the world at that time and *Phi Delta Kappan* had just named him as one of the top educators of the twentieth century. During a meeting in his office one day I asked him if he had any idea of the great significance of his contributions and the profound influence his work had on education at all levels.

"To tell you the truth," he said, "I did have the sense that my work had gained a certain level of prominence when I discovered that my name was an answer to a question on the National Teachers' Examination."

"Really?" I asked? "That's fantastic!"

"Well, I'm not sure, Tom, that I would consider it 'fantastic,'" he continued. "You see, I was the wrong answer to the question. . . ."

Remembering his expression and the gleam in his eyes as he related this tale, which I am sure is true, always makes me smile.

Chapter 41

"The 2 Sigma Problem"

Thomas R. Guskey

Today Ben's work would probably be described as "cutting edge," "forward thinking," "out of the box," and "pushing the envelope." There is little doubt that he thought about educational issues and approached educational problems differently than did most of his contemporaries. He was uncommonly tenacious and held on to problems longer than others. He also had an uncanny way of mentally turning problems around to view them from all possible angles.

Another of Ben's unique traits, however, was the extraordinary effort he took to engage others in this probing and analyzing process. On numerous occasions during his career he assembled groups of scholars to discuss problems, debate ideas, and seek meaningful solutions. His work on the *Taxonomy of Educational Objectives* (Bloom, Engelhart, Furst, Hill, & Krathwohl, 1956), *Compensatory Education for Cultural Deprivation* (Bloom, Davis, & Hess, 1965), and the International Association for the Evaluation of Educational Achievement (IEA) are but a few examples of this kind of special effort.

Likewise in his writing, Ben frequently challenged other researchers to join him in addressing what he considered to be a particularly pressing problem in education. He would begin by describing what was known about the problem, then point out several possible directions for the research, and finally challenge others to come up with different options or alternative solutions. Perhaps the best example of this is his work on the "2 Sigma Problem" (Bloom, 1984a, 1984b).

Ben described this problem by first presenting the work of two of his doctoral students, Joanne Anania (1981, 1983), and Arthur Burke (1983). In their dissertation research, Anania and Burke compared student learning under three different instructional conditions. The first was *conventional instruction* in which students were taught in group-based classes that included about thirty students and where periodic assessments were given mainly for the purposes of grading. The second was *mastery learning*, where students again were taught in group-based classes of about thirty students. While instruction was much the same in these classes, students were administered regular "formative" assessments for feedback, followed by individualized corrective instruction and parallel second assessments to determine the extent to which they mastered specific learning goals. The third condition was *tutoring*, where a good tutor was paired with each student. Tutored students were also administered regular formative assessments, along with corrective procedures and parallel second assessments, although the need for corrective work under tutoring was usually quite modest.

Students were randomly assigned to the three learning conditions, and their initial aptitude, interests, and previous achievement in the subject were all similar. The amount of time for instruction was the same in all three groups except for the corrective work in the mastery learning and tutoring groups.

The differences in students' final achievement under these three conditions were striking. Using the standard deviation (sigma) of the control (conventional) class as the measure of difference, Ben's students discovered that:

> The average student under tutoring was about two standard deviations above the average of the control class (the average tutored student was above 98 percent of the students in the control class). The average student under mastery learning was about one standard deviation above the average of the control class (the average mastery learning student was above 84 percent of the students in the control class). . . . Thus under the best learning conditions we can devise (tutoring), the average student is 2 sigma above the average control student taught under conventional group methods of instruction. (Bloom, 1984a, p. 4)

These differences are illustrated in the figure below and also provided the basis for Ben's "2 Sigma Problem":

> The tutoring process demonstrates that *most* students do have the potential to reach this high level of learning. I believe an important task of research and instruction is to seek ways of accomplishing this under more practical and realistic conditions than the one-to-one tutoring, which is too costly for most societies to bear on a large scale. This is the "2 Sigma" problem. Can researchers and teachers devise teaching-learning conditions that will enable the majority of students under *group instruction* to attain levels of achievement that can at present be reached only under tutoring conditions? (Bloom, 1984a, pp. 4–5)

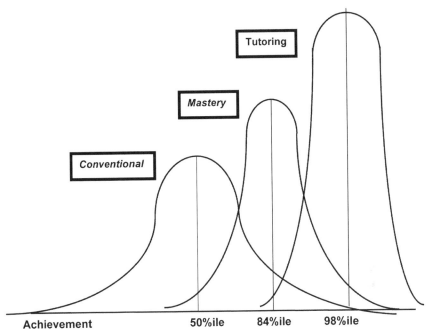

Achievement distributions for students under conventional, mastery learning, and tutorial instruction (Bloom, 1984a).

To Ben, the results from this research showed that virtually all students can learn to a very high level. The only exception might be children with severe learning disabilities, who compose perhaps 10 percent or less of current student populations. Accomplishing such a high level of learning through tutoring, however, would require a level of investment in education approximately twenty times higher than what is typical at the present time. Ben considered this both impractical and unrealistic. The challenge as he saw it, and as he hoped others would, was to find methods of group instruction that could yield similar results.

In his description of the 2 sigma problem, Ben also presented the work of several other of his students who were engaged in studies addressing this challenge, particularly the work of Levin (1979), Nordin (1979), Mevarech (1980), Tenenbaum (1982), and Leyton (1983). The results from these investigations showed that attaining this high level of achievement would probably require more than just improvements in the quality of group instruction. Researchers and teachers might also need to find ways of improving students' learning processes, the curriculum and instructional materials, the home environmental support of students' school learning, and a focus on higher-level thinking skills. Ben was convinced, however, that if one solution could be found, there would soon be a great many solutions.

Despite the obvious challenge, Ben and his students found the 2 sigma problem intriguing because the goal was so clear: to find methods of group instruction as effective as one-to-one tutoring. What remained was for researchers and practitioners to take up the challenge, to explore factors within the teaching-learning processes that they control, and then to find ways of altering those factors in order to help all students learn well. Ben stressed that this would not be easy, but it was also not impossible. The research of Anania and Burke demonstrated that, indeed, nearly all students can learn well. The challenge of the 2 sigma problem was to find ways of accomplishing this practically, efficiently, and economically.

Indeed, since Ben put forth this challenge, many researchers have investigated possible solutions that, even though not reaching the 2 sigma level of improvement, have made important contributions. Ben's article from *Educational Researcher* (Bloom, 1984a) has been cited in nearly 1500 research articles and publications. It also has been the basis of many modern research syntheses, notably the following works:

Ambrose, S. A., Bridges, M. W., DiPietro, M., Lovett, M. C., & Norman, M. K. (2010). *How learning works: Seven research-based principles for smart teaching.* San Francisco, CA: Jossey-Bass.

Hattie, J. (2009). *Visible learning: A synthesis of over 800 meta-analyses relating to achievement.* New York, NY: Routledge.

Wiliam, D. (2010). An integrative summary of the research literature and implications for a new theory of formative assessment. In H. L. Andrade & G. J. Cizek (Eds.), *Handbook of Formative Assessment* (pp. 18–40). New York, NY: Routledge.

Chapter 42

Always Consider the Audience

Lorin W. Anderson and Thomas R. Guskey

Ben was a devoted and studied writer who continually worked hard to improve his writing skills. He believed that writing brought clarity to thinking and did his best to ensure that readers clearly understood whatever it was that he was trying to communicate. This led him to be quite particular about where his work was published. Every article and book chapter was written with a special audience in mind, and he crafted his writing to convey his message to that specific group. He then sent his work to the journal or publisher that he believed would best reach his intended audience.

As his career advanced, Ben became more and more interested in sharing his ideas with the broadest audience possible. As a result, he published less in refereed research journals and more in educational "magazines" such as *Educational Leadership, Phi Delta Kappan,* and *Teacher*. When I asked him about this, he explained his rationale quite simply. "Our best and most prestigious research journals reach an audience of nine or ten thousand readers," he said. "A magazine like *Educational Leadership*, however, is sent to 180,000 educators each month. For ideas to influence educators, they must know about them—and this is a great way let them know about my ideas."

Lorin Anderson, former professor of education at the University of South Carolina and former student of Ben's, saw a classic example of this from Ben in 1987. Here is his story:

"One day Ben called me quite excited and asked, 'Lorin, do you subscribe to *Psychology Today?'*

"'No I don't,' I answered. 'But I'm sure I can get a copy. Why? What's in *Psychology Today?'*

"'There's an article about me in the April issue,' Ben replied. 'It's subtitled, "The Man Who Would Gladly Ruin American Education."'

"'That doesn't sound very flattering,' I said. 'What is it? A hatchet job?'

"'Never mind the title,' said Ben. 'The circulation is *300,000*! Just think, my message is getting out to 300,000 people!'

"It turned out that the article was not a hatchet job at all. In fact, it was highly complimentary of Ben and his work. The reason for the subtitle was explained on the first page of the article's text. Writer Paul Chance related:

> Much of the current back-to-basic movement in education is a revolt against the kinds of changes Bloom and like-minded people have tried to bring about. Bloom thinks, for example, that there is too much drill, too much rote learning, too little active participation by students, too much emphasis on lower-level "basic" skills, too much attention to "minimum" standards, too much competition and, most of all, too much failure in today's schools. He believes that the current educational system is structurally flawed and should be thoroughly rehabilitated, like an old house that is in danger of collapsing and killing its occupants. In this sense, Bloom would gladly plead guilty to having tried to "ruin" American education. (Chance, 1987, p. 43)

"Ben's concern was with making a difference in education and in our society at large. To do that he realized that he had to 'get the word out' to as many people involved in education as possible. So he wrote for varied audiences, targeting his message to those he believed could best make use of it. Many elements in the educational reforms that have taken place over the years and continue today are the result of Ben's efforts to do just that."

Chapter 43

You Are a Student
of Benjamin Bloom?

Joanne Anania

Ben's work influenced educators in all parts of the world. Translations of his books, many of which were published in over twenty different languages, lined the bookshelves of his home. His efforts in developing the International Association for the Evaluation of Educational Achievement (IEA) further extended his reputation among educational leaders worldwide. And deserving or not, the profound reverence and respect he garnered was often extended to his students. Joanne Anania, professor of education at Roosevelt University and former student of Ben's, learned about this in a most unusual way:

"In October 2000, my husband, Michael, and I traveled to southern Italy so that Michael could complete research on a book about his family. We spent a couple of days in the port of Naples, from where Michael's grandfather had departed for America in the early 1900s, and then drove to the region of Calabria and the small, isolated town of Adami. Through family stories I had heard from Michael, I imagined Adami to be an Italian version of one of the small Texas towns I had known as a child—dusty, brown, flat, and sparsely populated. I soon discovered, however, that except for the sparsely populated part, my image was completely mistaken.

"Knowing my aversion to curvy mountain roads, steep inclines, and suspension bridges, Michael abandoned thoughts of taking the scenic route through the mountains and decided instead to travel via the Autostrada del Sole, assuring me it would be just like an American superhighway. Shortly after leaving Naples, however, we discovered that the Autostrada traverses mountain peaks with only occasional relief provided by tunnels that go through the mountains. I survived the trip by keeping my eyes on the road and never looking sideways where either the mountain rose above us or the valley dropped below.

"When we finally left the Autostrada high in the Italian mountains, I took comfort in the belief that the worst part of the trip was behind us. But after a leisurely drive through several small towns, the road narrowed and began ascending even higher mountains. As we approached the town of Decollatora and the only hotel near Adami, the road spiraled around several steep mountains with no more than ten or fifteen meters between one sharp curve and the next. Discovering that Adami actually sat at the very top of a mountain, I resolved not to make the trip down the mountain again until the time came for us to leave for the airport.

"One evening during our visit, Michael and I met with his cousin, Raffelle, who served as the district's supervisor of schools. Raffelle told us that he needed to make a brief stop the next day at his office in Catanzaro, which was down the mountain and up another one. After that, however, he explained that he would be free to show us around the town.

"My anxious expression and the frightened tone in my voice must have made it clear that I was not pleased about traveling the steep and curvy mountain roads again. Sensing my apprehension, Raffelle did his best to calm my fears, addressing me in soothing tones that are usually reserved for the very sick and the very young, all the while moving his hands in a slow and easy motion. He also promised to drive slowly and very cautiously, repeating again and again, '*piano*' (slowly). His wife, Maria, laughed softly and whispered to Michael in Italian, 'Raffelle never does anything slowly.'

"The trip down the mountain the next day was not especially fast, but neither was it *piano*. Adding to my distress, we did not begin our trip back up the mountain until well after dark. Sitting in the backseat I could see little of the unlit road that took us spiraling upward, but I could feel the sharpness of the curves with every turn the car made. In my nervous state I also paid little attention to the conversation in Italian between Michael and Raffelle in the front seat until I heard Michael mention 'The University of Chicago.' He then turned to me and explained that Raffelle's doctorate was awarded by the University of Bologna, and he had asked about my doctorate. Since we shared the same field of study, Raffelle was curious about the content of my graduate studies.

"Being uncomfortable with the speed at which we were traveling and the treacherousness of the road, I managed only a couple of broad statements that Michael translated for Raffelle. After a continued exchange in Italian, Michael turned to me again and said, 'He wants to know who you studied with.' Fearing that at any moment we might fail to negotiate one of the tight mountain curves and plunge to our deaths, I was in no mood to carry on a conversation. But gathering my strength, I finally responded, 'Ask Raffelle if he's heard of Benjamin Bloom.'

"As Michael finished his translation with 'Benjamin Bloom,' both of Raffelle's hands flew off the steering wheel and upward toward the car's roof as he shouted, 'Benjamin Bloom!' Open mouthed, I stared straight ahead into the darkness beyond the headlights as Raffelle turned away from the winding road to look at me. Extending his right hand into the rear of the car, while the left continued its grasping gestures toward the car roof or perhaps the heavens, he continued, 'Benjamin Bloom! Benjamin Bloom!' I screamed, imagining the car careening down the mountainside, the sound of the crash accompanied by Raffelle's enthusiastic shouts of 'Benjamin Bloom! Benjamin Bloom!' Michael, surprised by the unexpected reaction, grabbed for the steering wheel to keep the car on the road and avoid a certain wreck.

"At long last we reached the top of the mountain and the town of Adami. Raffelle unlocked the door to his house and led Michael and me up the marble stairs to where his wife, Maria, was waiting. With great animation he announced to Maria that I had been a student of Benjamin Bloom. Maria looked at me with a newfound sense of admiration and affection. No longer was I welcomed merely because our husbands were cousins. Suddenly, I had become a person of note—a student of Benjamin Bloom. Maria approached me, hugged me as if for the first time, and asked Michael if this was, indeed, true. Michael simply smiled and nodded.

"Raffelle then disappeared into his study to search for his copies of Ben's books, but returned empty handed and clearly disappointed. Maria reminded him that he had loaned the books to one of his colleagues some time ago. This came as a great relief to me, of course. I envisioned being asked to autograph each copy, 'To Raffelle Anania with best wishes, [signed] A Student of Benjamin Bloom.' For the remainder of our stay in Adami, Raffelle's introductions of me to university-educated relatives and colleagues were always accompanied by 'a student of Benjamin Bloom.'

"Stories in Adami, Italy, are part of a rich oral history, remembered and passed from generation to generation. I am convinced that those stories today include, 'Once a student of Benjamin Bloom came to Adami. . . .'"

Chapter 44

A Sensitive Mentor

David Krathwohl

Although Ben had the reputation of being extremely demanding and very pointed in his criticism, he was also unusually sensitive to the feelings of those around him. He frequently took charge in meetings or discussions when he sensed the tone growing negative or overly personal, redirecting the conversation to focus attention on the professional issues at hand. If Ben ever believed that a colleague or student felt embarrassed or belittled, he would immediately intervene to calm their anxiety, often by making light of the situation.

One such occurrence took place during a conference held in Ben's honor at the University of Chicago just prior to his official retirement. David Krathwohl, former professor and dean of education at Syracuse University, was there and offered the following story about the occasion. David was also a former student of Ben's and one of the coauthors of the *Taxonomy of Educational Objectives* (Bloom, Engelhart, Furst, Hill, & Krathwohl, 1956).

"The conference in Ben's honor involved a series of invited speakers who reflected on the significance of different aspects of Ben's work. In the course of the presentations, Lee Shulman, then a professor of education at Stanford University, who had worked with Ben during his graduate studies at the University of Chicago, was talking about the impact of Ben's work on stimulated recall (Bloom, 1953c; 1954b). I was sitting next to Ben in the audience at the time.

"During his presentation, Lee mentioned some work that Norman Kagan and I had published while I was a faculty member at Michigan State University. We used videotape equipment to record clinical counseling and learning sessions, occasionally stopping the tape to have our informants relate what was going through their minds (see Kagan, Krathwohl, & Miller, 1963). Lee went on to note that while the technique was identical to the stimulated recall procedures Ben developed, his originating work was never cited.

"I, of course, was terribly embarrassed to have this pointed out in front of such a distinguished audience and especially in front of Ben. Were he a lesser man, Ben would have delighted in the revelation and taken solace in the fact that this professional snub had been recognized. But he didn't. Instead, Ben took note of my embarrassment, turned to me, and whispered, 'That's all right. I stole ideas from my major professor too.'

"To this day I have no idea whether Ben actually did that or not, and I seriously doubt that he ever did. But I never forgot how thoughtful it was of him to respond so quickly and so kindly in order to set me at ease. I also realized how typical it was of Ben to react in exactly that way, being more concerned about the feelings of others than about his own pride or recognition. His kindness was limitless and unmistakable."

Chapter 45

Different Approaches to Understanding

Thomas R. Guskey

It is said that all great minds have their quirks, and Ben was no exception. He always made special efforts to ensure that everyone with whom he spoke understood precisely what he was trying to communicate. But occasionally, those well-intentioned efforts got the best of him.

Being keenly aware that different individuals learn through different means, Ben always went out of his way to accommodate those differences in his teaching. Every class that he taught included a variety of learning activities and typically involved peer tutoring or other forms of cooperative learning.

Even in conference presentations to large audiences, Ben did his best to incorporate a variety of presentation formats. At first he used prepared transparencies displayed on an overhead projector to visually communicate the ideas he presented orally. But then Sophie, Ben's wife and a keen observer of audiences, suggested to him that while helpful, the transparencies were not particularly engaging. So Ben began carrying blank transparencies and colored markers with him to presentations and would use these to draw models and illustrations of his theories as he spoke. Although this was a bit more engaging, coordinating the use of transparencies, pens, microphones, and lecture notes often proved difficult.

One idiosyncrasy noted by many of Ben's students involved similar efforts to communicate over the phone. Often during meetings in his office in Judd Hall, Ben would receive a telephone call from a reporter or educator in another part of the country or another part of the world. Not wanting to put off the caller, he would excuse himself from the conversation with the student, indicating that he would not be long but that the call required his immediate attention. He then would proceed to explain some aspect of his theories or research to the caller, always with animated enthusiasm.

This happened during one of our many conversations. Ben answered a phone call and, after excusing himself to me, began to explain some aspect of his work to an education reporter from the *New York Times*. At one point in their conversation it became obvious that the reporter was just not grasping what Ben was trying to communicate. After three or four unsuccessful attempts to clarify his meaning, Ben rose from his chair, turned to the blackboard, and said, "Look, it's like this . . ." and proceeded to illustrate his point on the board. Although this may not have been particularly helpful to the caller, observing the process showed me an especially human side of Ben that still, today, makes me smile.

Chapter 46

Developing Talent
in Young People

Lauren Sosniak and Thomas R. Guskey

One of Ben's last major research endeavors was the Development of Talent Project. This large-scale investigation involved the detailed study of 120 individuals who, although relatively young (under thirty-five years of age), had realized exceptional levels of accomplishment in their chosen field. Six different fields of endeavor were selected for investigation: two involving academic/intellectual talent (mathematics and neurological research), two involving artistic talent (sculpture and concert piano), and two involving athletic/psychomotor talent (swimming and tennis).

Data for the project were drawn from in-depth interviews with approximately twenty talented men and women in each field, as well as from interviews with their parents. The goal was to search for recurrent patterns in the backgrounds and educational histories of these accomplished individuals in the hope that such consistencies might shed light on how the development of such extraordinary talent was achieved (Bloom, 1985).

The Development of Talent Project extended Ben's earlier research in two important ways. First, his work on mastery learning and the 2 sigma problem focused on methods of teaching that would enable nearly all students to a reach a high level of achievement. In the Development of Talent Project, however, he pushed even further, exploring the very upper limits of knowledge, skill, and accomplishment. The issue for Ben was not simply how students might be helped to reach high levels of learning in individual courses. It was now to discover how children and youth eventually reach the pinnacle of adult accomplishment.

Second, the Development of Talent Project also broadened Ben's earlier work on alterable variables—factors that educators can influence to improve students' learning. Throughout his career Ben emphasized the importance of alterable variables in educational environments. He made his position particularly clear in a letter to the editors of the *Harvard Educational Review*, critiquing a study by Arthur Jensen:

> While the psychologist and the geneticist may wish to speculate about how to improve the gene pool, the educator cannot and should not. The educator must be an environmentalist, bridled or unbridled. It is through the environment that he must fashion the educational process. Learning takes place within the child; the educator therefore, tries to influence this learning by providing the appropriate environment. If heredity imposes limits, then so be it. The educator must work with whatever is left, whether it is 20 percent of the variance or 50 percent. . . . The improvement of education and other environments is really the only means available to a civilized society for the improvement of the lot and the fate of humankind. (Bloom, quoted in Sosniak, 2001, p. 2)

As his work on alterable variables evolved, Ben pushed even further. He shifted his focus from general characteristics of educational environments to specific teaching and learning variables—those that are alterable either before the teaching-learning process begins, or as part of the process itself. To Ben, the study of alterable variables was central to educational improvement efforts. Such a focus "enables researchers to move from an emphasis on prediction and classification to . . . new ways of understanding, explaining, and altering human learning" (Bloom, 1980a, p. 385).

These premises provided the foundation for the Development of Talent Project. Ben speculated that in every society there exists an enormous pool of talent that can be either developed or wasted, depending in large measure on environmental conditions that are alterable. By studying persons who, by the age of thirty-five, had demonstrated the highest level of accomplishment in their selected fields, he hoped to discover how these individuals were discovered, encouraged, and otherwise helped to develop. If alterable variables could be found that contributed to this exceptional level of achievement, perhaps many more individuals could be helped to reach similar levels of accomplishment.

The results of the project confirmed what many scholars had suspected: developing exceptional talent takes a lot of time. As Ben stressed in the introductory chapter:

> The study has provided strong evidence that no matter what the initial characteristics (or gifts) of the individuals, unless there is a long and intensive process of encouragement, nurturance, education, and training, the individuals will not attain extreme levels of capability in their particular fields. (Bloom, 1985, p. 3)

Internationally recognized concert pianists, for example, worked for an average of seventeen years from their first formal lessons to their first international competition.

How these talented individuals spent their time was equally important. In their early years of learning, only a small amount of time was spent in formal instruction—perhaps only an hour or two, once a week. Most of their time was spent more informally, playing in related activities; demonstrating their talent to friends and relatives; and reading, watching, or listening to others involved in the talent area. These early experiences were fun, engaging, and supported by those around them. Only after they developed their own interest in the area did they realize the value of precision and refinement in their work. They also began to see value in their area because they witnessed others in their family and community engaging in the same or related areas. The development of their talent was a learning process for these individuals, interwoven in the activities of their everyday lives.

The social context in which their talent developed was also important. All of these individuals developed their talent in an environment that offered support, encouragement, advice, insight, guidance, and goodwill of many others. In many ways, it was the result of many people working for the accomplishments of one.

Related to this social context was their involvement and active participation in "communities of practice" for their respective fields. Communities of practice are groups of people who share a common interest and are willing to invest substantial time and energy to work in that area. Communities of practice may inhabit a physical place or they may be "virtual," connecting people through writing, radio, television, the Internet, social media, or some other form of technology.

For most individuals in the Development of Talent Project, families were their first community of practice. Typically they grew up in homes where that activity was valued and admired. The parents of these talented individuals were rarely involved professionally in that area, but still had an active interest in the field or a closely related activity. Although working as accountants, salespersons, lawyers, or fruit vendors, they loved science, music, or sports. As a consequence, their children were regularly exposed to activities connected with the talent area. These activities provided an interest, amusement, a source of entertainment for parents and their children to share.

As these talented individuals got older, they began to enter communities of practice outside the home. Young scientists had backyard or basement pals with whom they studied the ecology of their area or conducted experiments with chemicals found in youth science sets. Concert pianists began lessons with a local music teacher and typically became members of a group of students involved in small recitals once or twice a year.

Swimmers took lessons at the local "Y" or community pool and eventually joined groups of swimmers in local swim clubs.

Not all the findings from the Development of Talent Project were expected, however. Ben and his team initially believed that these exceptionally talented individuals would be identified early on as possessing special gifts or qualities in their talent area. This early recognition would then lead to the provision of special instruction and encouragement. But the team soon discovered that this assumption of early discovery followed by instruction and support was wrong.

The individuals included in the Development of Talent Project typically did *not* show unusual promise at the start. And, in most cases, there was no early intention of working toward a standard of excellence in a particular field. Ben emphasized, "This research has raised questions about earlier views of special gifts and innate aptitudes as necessary prerequisites of talent development" (Bloom, 1985, p. 3). Instead these individuals were encouraged and supported in their learning—both formally and informally—before they were identified as "special." As they spent more time and developed greater interest in the talent area they became "identified" as having special qualities that, in turn, were rewarded with more encouragement and support. Aptitudes, attitudes, and expectations grew in concert with one another, and were mutually confirming. As Ben once told a reporter in regard to the project: "We were looking for exceptional kids and what we found were exceptional conditions" (Bloom, quoted in Sosniak, 2001, p. 5).

With the Development of Talent Project, Ben took on a study of considerable methodological complexity. He worked doggedly to understand what we frequently refer to as "the limits of learning." He marveled at the lives and learning of the talented individuals who were included in the study. But perhaps most importantly, he raised new ideas about time, tasks, and the social contexts for learning that provide the challenges for the next generations of scholars. Ben summarized these challenges in the final chapter:

> All of this is to point to the enormous human potential available in each society and the likelihood that only a very small amount of this human potential is ever fully developed. We believe that each society could vastly increase the amount and kinds of talent it develops. We hope that this book has provided some clues as to the positive conditions necessary for such talent development. (Bloom, 1985, p. 549)

Since its publication, *Developing Talent in Young People* (Bloom, 1985) has had profound influence on research in the areas of school improvement, creativity, gifted education, and the development of talent in sports and the performing arts, as evidenced in the following publications:

Creech, A., & Hallam, S. (2011). Learning a musical instrument: The influence of interpersonal interaction on outcomes for school-aged pupils. *Psychology of Music, 39*(1), 102–122.

Gilbert, W., & Hamel, T. (2011). Enhancing coach-parent relationships in youth sports: Increasing harmony and minimizing hassle. *International Journal of Sports Science and Coaching, 6*(1), 37–42.

Kilgore, S. B., & Reynolds, K. J. (2011). *From silos to success: Reframing schools for success.* Thousand Oaks, CA: Corwin Press.

Morawska, A., & Sanders, M. R. (2009). Parenting gifted and talented children: Conceptual and empirical foundations. *Gifted Child Quarterly, 53*(3), 163–173.

Starko, A. J. (2010). *Creativity in the classroom: Schools of curious delight* (4th ed.). New York, NY: Routledge.

Chapter 47

New Views of "Giftedness"

Judy Eby

As noted earlier, Ben was a staunch environmentalist and felt strongly that any true educator had to be. He recognized, of course, that genetic factors make individuals different at birth. Nevertheless, he was convinced that those differences are small compared to the tremendous variation among individuals attributable to differences in environmental factors. His beliefs about the powerful influence of the environment stemmed largely from his hallmark research in developing *Stability and Change in Human Characteristics* (Bloom, 1964a) and continued to be reflected in all of his work, including his later study, *Developing Talent in Young People* (Bloom, 1985).

Judy Eby, a former student of Ben's at Northwestern University, shared many of his beliefs about environmental influences. She offered the following story:

"In the early 1980s, I was the coordinator of gifted education in a school district in the northwest suburbs of Chicago. The state of Illinois had mandated that all school districts provide gifted education programs and had arbitrarily established that the top 5 percent of students in each school district were to be enrolled. I found this quite disturbing because it meant that whether or not a child was considered 'gifted' depended on where the child lived. A child living in one district might be labeled gifted, but if she moved across the street to another district she might be excluded from the program. In the district where I worked, a fifth grade boy who scored at the 96th percentile on a standardized achievement test was included in the program and labeled 'gifted,' while his twin brother who scored at the 94th percentile was not.

"I believed this system of selection and exclusion was detestable and counter to what I considered sound educational policy. Whatever 'giftedness' was, it certainly could not be defined by a single, standardized test. So I began experimenting with a system that allowed students to 'self-select' for the gifted program with no reliance on pencil-and-paper tests. Instead, I created curriculum units and instructed all students in the school on how they could apply to be in the gifted program. Each curriculum unit had a pre-task that students completed and turned in as their application for that part of the program. The result was that what the students considered 'gifted' differed with each curriculum unit. The program met with great success and was described in two different articles that I developed for *Educational Leadership* (Eby, 1983, 1984).

"Shortly after the articles appeared, I learned of Benjamin Bloom's work on talent development and wrote to him requesting more information about his studies. He wrote back indicating that he had 'encountered' my articles and thought that I was 'definitely on the right track.' He also invited me to meet with him at Northwestern University where he was then teaching after having retired from his faculty position at the University of Chicago.

"Our meeting turned out to be one of the most intellectually exhilarating experiences I had ever known. I shared with Mr. Bloom my frustrations in trying to work with school administrators, gifted program coordinators, and teachers who seemed set on using achievement tests for identifying students for gifted programs. Without a numerical score, these educators believed that schools would be inundated with parents trying to get their 'not truly gifted' children included in the program.

"After listening to my stories, Mr. Bloom responded that he thought my take on these issues was quite accurate, and that evidence from his most recent studies confirmed my perceptions. Regarding the administrators who wanted to rely solely on pencil-and-paper tests for identifying gifted students, he responded, 'These are clearly the type of methods that are used by nongifted people trying to identify the gifted.' His honesty and candor surprised me, but also renewed my commitment to view 'giftedness' from a much broader perspective.

"The encouragement Mr. Bloom offered spurred me to continue my own studies of giftedness. I became one of his last graduate students, completing my dissertation research at Northwestern University on creating an operational definition of gifted behavior and showing that these behaviors can be developed in most individuals through experiential learning opportunities."

Chapter 48

Subtle Humor

Lauren Sosniak

Ben was extremely quick-witted with a sense of humor that sometimes bordered on "parched." Often in conversation he would make brief, extraordinarily funny comments that passed unnoticed by those not paying close attention. Those familiar with Ben's style, however, were constantly amused. Lauren Sosniak, former professor of education at San Jose State University and who, as a student, worked closely with Ben in the early 1980s on the Development of Talent Project (Bloom, 1985), shared the following example:

"One day Ben and I were driving together on Lake Shore Drive from the University of Chicago campus to a meeting on North Michigan Avenue in downtown Chicago. Our work together on the Talent Project had just begun and, not knowing Ben very well, I felt uncomfortable initiating conversation. So for most of the drive, neither one of us said very much.

"Suddenly a dilapidated old car cut in front of us using no signal, causing Ben to hit the brakes hard. Being so close to the vehicle, I noticed that the license plate read 'IQ 200,' but said nothing about it. Ben, obviously noticing too, turned to me and asked, 'Do you suppose that's for a family of four?'

"Quite surprised but completely amused, I burst out laughing. It was a perfect line delivered subtly but with great timing. It eased the tension between us and set the stage for the many conversations we shared afterward in our work together on the Talent Project."

Chapter 49

Students Come First

Jeffrey K. Smith

As so many stories in this book reveal, Ben was completely dedicated to his students. None doubted that he was a demanding taskmaster and unyielding in his insistence on excellence. But he was also exceptionally kind and giving in ways that many of his students found quite extraordinary. The following story, offered by Jeffry K. Smith, professor of education and codirector of the Education Assessment Research Unit at the University of Otago in Dunedin, New Zealand, illustrates this quality of Ben's quite well.

"One day, while standing in line together to purchase a cup of coffee in Judd Hall on the University of Chicago campus, Ben turned to me and asked how I was getting on. I told him that things were going well, but that I had recently lost my reading glasses and needed to get a new pair. Upon hearing this, Ben immediately took off his glasses and offered them to me. 'Here, try these,' he said. 'I've got another pair and you can borrow them until you can replace yours.'

"Most readers do not know me, but I am at least twice the size of Ben. His glasses would not make it back to my ears, much less reach over them. And Ben actually *needed* glasses. I needed only mild magnification to make reading a bit easier. Still, that didn't matter. What mattered was that one of his students needed glasses and he had an extra pair.

"To this day, I try to keep that same perspective: What can I do to help my students be successful? I got that from Ben, and it has always held me in good stead."

Chapter 50

Unique Traveling Rituals

Roy Phillips

As one of the founding fathers of the International Association for the Evaluation of Educational Achievement (IEA), Ben traveled extensively to work with educators in the participating countries. His central role in the development of the IEA Six-Subject Survey and in the initiation of the Second International Mathematics Study (SIMS) further extended his travels. While this work and the associated travel were difficult and tiring, Ben never lost enthusiasm for it, largely due to the close personal friendships he developed with educational leaders throughout the world.

One of those friendships was with Roy W. Phillips, who at that time served as assistant director of the Curriculum Development Division in the New Zealand Department of Education. Roy was the person responsible for persuading the New Zealand Department of Education to join IEA. He hoped that through IEA membership New Zealand might develop useful baseline data to judge the success of their newly developed curricula. Roy offered the following story:

"Although I did not meet Ben Bloom until 1968 at an IEA meeting in Stockholm, Sweden, I was already quite familiar with many aspects of his work. The *Taxonomy of Educational Objectives* (Bloom, Engelhart, Furst, Hill, & Krathwohl, 1956) had provided the foundation for our newly developed science curriculum in New Zealand.

"At my invitation, Ben visited New Zealand the following year where we worked together on curriculum development for courses in New Zealand's primary and secondary schools. In very short time Ben became both my mentor and personal inspiration. We remained close friends from that time on and frequently traveled together. These experiences gave me unique insights into a highly personal side of Ben that I am confident few persons apart from his family ever knew.

"I discovered that Ben had distinctive rituals for traveling that allowed him to keep things well under control and to avoid many of the hassles associated with worldwide travel. I noticed, for example, that Ben would carry only a small suitcase and briefcase which, whenever possible, he kept with him at all times to avoid checking any luggage with the airlines. When we arrived at our hotel room, Ben would upend the contents of the suitcase into a single drawer. From that one drawer he would service all of his personal needs during our entire visit, always looking quite dapper and well groomed. When it came time to leave, Ben would simply reverse the process, dumping the entire contents of the drawer back into his suitcase. This left me wondering, of course, what Ben's wife, Sophie, thought when Ben and his suitcase with its disheveled contents arrived back home.

"The first time I experienced Ben's unique travel rituals was on a trip to Melbourne, Australia, in 1972. One evening after taking part in an IEA seminar hosted by the Australian Council for Educational Research (ACER), Ben and I shared a taxi back to our hotel where Ben insisted that the night porter find us suitable beverages before retiring, tipping the porter generously for the service.

"Shortly after we retired to our respective rooms, my phone rang. Answering it I heard a somewhat muddled and barely audible voice asking me if I would agree to take over as the executive director of IEA in Stockholm. Thinking it was Ben playing a joke, I immediately telephoned Ben's room, suggesting that in the future we best abstain from such late-night libations. As it turned out, Ben was not the caller and the offer was in earnest. For his part, however, Ben had known about the impending invitation for some time, although he never mentioned it to me.

"Despite the lateness of the hour, Ben and I had a long conversation that night on the phone, discussing the vital role of international research organizations and IEA in particular. It was a conversation that I will always remember and one that served me well in my role as IEA's executive director.

"A year later Ben and I found ourselves together again, this time in New Orleans where a meeting of the IEA Standing Committee coincided with the annual meeting of the American Educational Research Association (AERA). Both of these meetings also coincided with the Mardi Gras celebration in New Orleans. Ben convinced me that I needed to experience Mardi Gras firsthand, so the two of us set out from our hotel to observe a Mardi Gras parade. I was unsuccessful at catching any of the aluminum doubloons thrown by parade participants, so Ben found a young fellow holding a fistful and bribed him with real currency to obtain a few souvenirs for me to take back to New Zealand.

"After the parade passed, Ben and I ventured on, traversing Decatur Street to Jackson Square, passing the St. Louis Cathedral and statue of General Jackson, and eventually arriving at Pat O'Brien's Tavern. Ben insisted that this was the place for me to experience a 'New Orleans Hurricane'—a dangerous concoction of several different types of rum with a small portion of fruit juice. Later we walked along Royal and Bourbon Streets, taking in the many ornate courtyards, restaurants, and the exotic sights, sounds, and odors of the nightlife of New Orleans.

"Although the hour was growing late, an untiring Ben insisted that no stay in New Orleans was complete without a visit to Preservation Hall, the mecca of New Orleans jazz. So we set out again. Once inside Preservation Hall, Ben found his way to the bandstand where a generous tip resulted in a stirring rendition of 'When the Saints Come Marching In.' It was a night I also will never forget. And despite the interests that brought Ben and me together, neither IEA nor educational research was mentioned once during the entire evening.

"On another occasion, Ben and I found ourselves together in Budapest, Hungary. Ben and Arieh Levy escorted me through the reconstructed Jewish Quarter of Budapest. It was from there during World War II that Arieh had escaped the Nazis dressed as a priest, and this was the first time he had returned to his homeland since the war. For both Ben and Arieh, the visit stirred deep feelings and memories of personal grief from the Holocaust. I, too, found myself overcome with emotion sharing that moment with them.

"Later during that same visit to Budapest, Ben and I walked past the home of Zoltán Kodály, who along with Béla Bartók and others had fathered a classical musical outburst in Hungary in the early part of the twentieth century. Shortly afterward in the foyer of the Országos Pedagógiai Intézet, we passed a bust of László Rátz, the renowned Hungarian mathematician and teacher. Rátz's students, many of whom immigrated to the United States, epitomized an era of Hungarian mathematical and scientific brilliance. Ben turned to me and asked, 'What is it about a nation that suddenly sees them produce such a rash of excellence—of top musicians, mathematicians, sportsmen and women, educators, and the like?' Realizing that this was not a rhetorical question and an answer was required, I mumbled a cursory response that offered few profound insights while Ben listened intently. Although the question was never resolved that night, I saw Ben's intense interest in it and realized he would not leave it unresolved. It wasn't until nearly two decades later, however, that Ben and his students launched a major research effort to discover the answer in their work on the Development of Talent Project (see Bloom, 1985).

"On another occasion in the mid-1970s, I had the opportunity to visit Ben at his home in Chicago, where he took me on a tour of Chicago's

South Side. Ben's heartfelt empathy for the plight of impoverished ethnic groups in the city (see Bloom, 1964b) and his hopes for the success of children's television programs such as *Sesame Street* truly impressed me. Later, as we walked around the University of Chicago campus, Ben pointed out the tremendous variety of architectural styles and the many renowned scholars who had made the University of Chicago their academic home. I saw clearly how proud Ben was to be part of that university community.

"At that time IEA was experiencing financial difficulties and its future was in doubt. Funding was difficult to find and some of the early supporters, having grown tired of the continual quest for research monies, were ready to let the organization die from lack of resources. I, however, believed strongly that it would be a shame to let this remarkable effort lapse. So with the help of a small grant from the McKenzie Foundation, I set out on one last quest to launch IEA into a second mathematics study. With Ben's help I developed a grant proposal that resulted in substantial financial support from the Spencer Foundation, and the Second International Mathematics Study (SIMS) was begun. I have no doubt, however, that Ben's assistance and support was primarily responsible for the application's success.

"A few years later I was able to return Ben's hospitality when I convinced him and Sophie to extend their visit to Australia to include a stopover in New Zealand as guests of the New Zealand Department of Education. Our time together included several meetings with various curriculum groups and gatherings of educational researchers. But mostly it was spent touring the New Zealand countryside, where Sophie took charge of the suitcases. As we visited the scenic towns of Christchurch, Queenstown, and my hometown of Dunedin, our conversations ranged from world affairs to local cuisine, but never touched on educational research. Although it reminded me of our time together in New Orleans, Bourbon Street seemed worlds away."

Chapter 51

A Productive Career

Thomas R. Guskey

After spending several years as a faculty member at the University of Kentucky and serving in several different administrative positions, I applied for and was offered the position of dean of education at another university. I was between projects, had grown frustrated with the research in which I was engaged, and looked upon this as an opportunity to make a different kind of contribution. It would bring new surroundings filled with new responsibilities and new challenges. It also meant a substantial increase in my modest salary as a professor. But before accepting the offer, I called my mentor and friend, Ben Bloom, to discuss the impending change.

Ben listened carefully as I described the position to him, the new challenges it would bring, and the contribution I believed I could make. He asked about the people with whom I would be working most closely and the kind of support I anticipated receiving from those in higher-level administrative positions. But all the while I sensed an underlying uneasiness in his voice. He was holding something back.

When we finished considering all the pros and cons of the new position and our conversation began to wind down, Ben suddenly became quiet. "Well, Ben," I interjected, "what do you think?"

"I think you have a very important decision to make here, Tom," he replied. "I believe it comes down to this: Do you want to have a productive career, or do you want to be a dean?"

His utter frankness took me by surprise. Ben had always been totally honest with me, but this was more direct and more conclusive than was typical even of him. It also left no doubt where he stood on such matters.

Ben valued the work of university administrators and understood what a crucial role they play in forming the character of an institution.

Furthermore, over the course of his career he often had been in a position similar to mine. On numerous occasions he, too, was offered high-level administrative positions at other universities, all at substantially higher pay and more benefits than he received as a faculty member at the University of Chicago. But after thorough consideration, he consistently turned them down.

To Ben's way of thinking, serving as a dean or other university administrator required time and a level of commitment that made it impossible to remain highly productive as a researcher, scholar, and teacher. A choice needed to be made, therefore, between one and the other—and for him, the choice had always been clear. His unapologetic advice helped clarify the choice for me as well. I remained a professor and researcher, with no regret.

Chapter 52

The Benjamin S. Bloom Dissertation Fellowship

Thomas R. Guskey

Ben's legacy lives on today at the University of Chicago through the Benjamin S. Bloom Dissertation Fellowship. This fellowship was funded initially from royalties earned from *Taxonomy of Educational Objectives, Handbooks 1 and 2* (Bloom, Engelhart, Furst, Hill, & Krathwohl, 1956; Krathwohl, Bloom, & Masia, 1964). With the help of David Krathwohl, the Hannah Hammond Professor Emeritus and former dean of the Graduate School of Education at Syracuse University, Sophie Bloom arranged for funds to be transferred to the University of Chicago to establish the fellowship. As described earlier, David was a former student of Ben's and one of the coauthors of *Taxonomy*.

The Benjamin S. Bloom Dissertation Fellowship is awarded each year to an outstanding doctoral candidate in any social science discipline at the University of Chicago whose dissertation research focuses on education or schooling. Its purpose is to support the research efforts of promising doctoral students interested in educational issues. It also ensures that Ben's legacy at the University of Chicago will long endure through the students that his work continues to support.

All royalties earned from this book are donated to the Benjamin S. Bloom Dissertation Fellowship.

Postscript

Thomas R. Guskey

While sorting through the materials that she kept on Ben, Sophie Bloom discovered an audiocassette recording of a presentation that he made on February 27, 1977. The presentation was entitled "Human Characteristics and School Learning," and described the premises of Ben's recently published book with the same name. This lecture was part of the "From the Midway" series, a weekly Public Broadcasting Service (PBS) program that featured lectures and discussions by faculty and guests of the University of Chicago. It began as the Woodward Court Resident Masters Lecture Series sponsored by Professor Izaak Wirszup and his wife, Pera.

Sophie gave the recording to her son, David, who owns the Bloom School of Jazz in Chicago. In his studio, David digitized the recording and sent it to me as a CD. Virginia Lacefield, technical support specialist in the Academic Technology Group at the University of Kentucky, helped me consider various options for making this recording available to those who purchased this book and were interested in hearing Ben discuss his work. Stuart Reedy, programmer systems leader in the Instructional Technology Center of the College of Education, University of Kentucky, then built the website that would allow access. The website is www.coe.uky.edu/Bloom/. The figure below is an illustration of the website. The College of Education, University of Kentucky, hosts and maintains this site.

Reactions to the website have been quite phenomenal. Numerous people have contacted me to tell me what a wonderful experience it is to be able to hear Ben talk so personally about his work. The only less-than-positive comment I have received came from Neville Postlethwaite, who told me that although he immensely enjoyed listening to the lecture, he considered it a bit haunting. It seemed to him that Ben was talking to him from heaven.

 College of Education
"Research and reflection for learning and leading"

Audio for *Benjamin S. Bloom: Portraits of an Educator*

Lecture split into two parts (approximately 30 minutes each)

Part 1 (28 MB)

Part 2 (27 MB)

Full lecture as single file (65 MB)

Hosting provided the University of Kentucky College of Education

College of Education
Copyright UK College of Education
Lexington, KY 40506 -- (859) 257-6076

Appendix A
Writings of Benjamin S. Bloom

Bloom, B. S. (1944). Some major problems in educational measurement. *Journal of Educational Research, 38*(2), 139–142.

Bloom, B. S. (1947a). Implications of problem-solving difficulties for instruction and remediation. *School Review, 55*(1), 45–49.

Bloom, B. S. (1947b). Testing in the study of educational progress. In *Exploring individual differences: A report of the 1947 Invitational Conference on Testing Problems* (entire volume). Washington, DC: American Council on Educational Studies.

Bloom, B. S. (1949). A taxonomy of educational objectives: Opening remarks of B. S. Bloom for the meeting of examiners at Monticello, IL, November 27, 1949. In D. R. Krathwohl (Ed.), *Summary report: College and university examiner's taxonomy conference*. Champaign, IL: Bureau of Research and Service, College of Education, University of Illinois (mimeographed).

Bloom, B. S., & Allison, J. M. (1949). Developing a college placement test program. *Journal of General Education, 3*(3), 210–215.

Bloom, B. S., & Allison, J. M. (1950). The operation and evaluation of a college placement program. *Journal of General Education, 4*(3), 221–233.

Bloom, B. S., & Broder, L. J. (1950). *Problem-solving processes of college students: An exploratory investigation*. Chicago, IL: University of Chicago Press.

Bloom, B. S., & Ward, F. C. (1952). The Chicago Bachelors of Arts degree after ten years. *Journal of Higher Education, 23*(4), 459–467.

Bloom, B. S. (1953a). Personality variables and classroom performance. *Journal of the National Association of Deans of Women, 16*(4).

Bloom, B. S. (1953b). Test reliability for what? *Journal of Educational Psychology, 45*(4), 517–526.

Bloom, B. S. (1953c). Thought processes in lectures and discussions. *Journal of General Education, 7*(3), 160–169.

Bloom, B. S. (1954a). Changing conceptions of examining at the University of Chicago. In P. Dressel (Ed.), *Evaluation in general education*. Dubuque, IA:

W. C. Brown Company. [Reprinted in Bloom, B. S. (1981). *All our children learning* (pp. 245–266). New York, NY: McGraw-Hill.]

Bloom, B. S. (1954b). Thought processes of students in discussion classes. In S. J. French (Ed.). *Accent on teaching: Experiments in general education.* New York, NY: Harper Brothers.

Bloom, B. S., Engelhart, M. D., Furst, E. J., Hill, W. H., & Krathwohl, D. R. (1956). *Taxonomy of educational objectives, Handbook 1: The cognitive domain.* New York, NY: McKay.

Bloom, B. S. & Heyns, I. V. (1956). Development and applications of tests of educational achievement. *Review of Educational Research, 26*(1), 72–88.

Stern, G. G., Stein, M. I., & Bloom, B. S. (1956). *Methods in personality assessment.* Glencoe, IL: Free Press.

Bloom, B. S. (1957). The 1955 normative study of the Tests of General Educational Development. *School Review, 64*(3), 110–124.

Bloom, B. S., & Statler, C. (1957). Changes in the states on the Tests of General Educational Development. *School Review, 65*(2), 202–221.

Bloom, B. S. (1958a). *Evaluation in secondary schools.* New Delhi, India: All India Council for Secondary Education.

Bloom, B. S. (1958b). Ideas, problems, and methods of inquiry. In P. Dressel (Ed.), *Integration of educational experiences.* Chicago, IL: University of Chicago Press.

Bloom, B. S., & Webster, H. (1960). The outcomes of college. *Review of Educational Research, 30*(3), 321–333.

Bloom, B. S. (1961a). *Evaluation in higher education.* New Delhi, India: University Grants Commission.

Bloom, B. S. (1961b). Quality control in education. *Tomorrow's teaching.* Oklahoma City, OK: Frontiers of Science Foundation, pp. 54–61.

Bloom, B. S., & Peters, F. (1961). *Use of academic prediction scales for counseling and selecting college entrants.* Glencoe, IL: Free Press.

Bloom, B. S. (1963a). Report on creativity research. In C. W. Taylor and F. X. Barron (Eds.) *Scientific creativity, its recognition and development.* New York, NY: Wiley and Sons.

Bloom, B. S. (1963b). Testing cognitive ability and achievement. In N. L. Gage (Ed.), *Handbook of research on teaching* (pp. 379–397). New York, NY: Rand McNally.

Bloom, B. S. (1964a). *Stability and change in human characteristics.* New York, NY: John Wiley & Sons.

Bloom, B. S. (1964b). *Research problems of education and cultural deprivation.* Based on working papers and suggestions contributed by participants in the Research Conference on Education and Cultural Deprivation, Chicago, IL (ERIC Document No. ED001715).

Krathwohl, D. R., Bloom, B. S., & Masia, B. B. (1964). *Taxonomy of educational objectives, Handbook 2: The affective domain.* New York, NY: McKay.

Bloom, B. S. (1965a). The role of the educational sciences in curriculum development. *International Journal of the Educational Sciences, 1*(1), 5–15.

Bloom, B. S. (1965b). *Early learning in the home.* Los Angeles, CA: University of California at Los Angeles (ERIC Document No. ED019127).

Bloom, B. S., Davis, A., & Hess, R. (1965). *Compensatory education for cultural deprivation.* New York, NY: Holt, Rinehart, and Winston.

Bloom, B. S. (1966a). The international study of educational achievement: Development of hypotheses. In P. Dressel (Ed.), *Proceedings of the 1965 Invitational Conference on Testing Problems.* Princeton, NJ: Educational Testing Service.

Bloom, B. S. (1966b). Peak learning experiences. In M. Provus (Ed.), *Innovations for time to teach.* Washington, DC: National Educational Association.

Bloom, B. S. (1966c). Stability and change in human characteristics: Implications for school reorganization. *Educational Administration Quarterly, 2*(1), 35–49.

Bloom, B. S. (1966d). Twenty-five years of educational research. *American Educational Research Journal, 3*(2), 211–221.

Bloom, B. S. (1967a). *Toward a theory of testing which includes measurement-evaluation-assessment.* Center for the Study of Evaluation of Instructional Programs, Occasional Report No. 9. Paper presented at the Symposium on Problems in the Evaluation of Instruction, Los Angeles, CA (ERIC Document No. ED036878).

Bloom, B. S. (Ed.) (1967b). Social factors in education. Chapter 5 in T. Husén (Ed.), *International study of achievement in mathematics: A comparison of twelve countries, Vol. II* (pp. 199–259). New York, NY: John Wiley & Sons.

Bloom, B. S., & Foshay, A. W. (1967). Formulation of hypotheses. Chapter 3 in T. Husén (Ed.), *International study of achievement in mathematics: A comparison of twelve countries, Vol. I* (pp. 64–75). New York, NY: John Wiley & Sons.

Bloom, B. S. (1968a). Learning for mastery. *UCLA Evaluation Comment, 1*(2), 1–12 (ERIC Document No. ED053419).

Bloom, B. S. (1968b). R & D centers: Promise and fulfillment. *Journal of Research and Development in Education, 1*(4), 101–113.

Bloom, B. S. (Ed.). (1969a). *Cross-national study of educational attainment: Stage 1 of the IEA investigation in six subject areas. Final report, volume I.* Washington, DC: U. S. Department of Health, Education, and Welfare (ERIC Document No. ED034290).

Bloom, B. S. (Ed.). (1969b). *Cross-national study of educational attainment: Stage 1 of the IEA investigation in six subject areas. Final report, volume II.* Washington, DC: U. S. Department of Health, Education, and Welfare (ERIC Document No. ED034300).

Bloom, B. S. (1969c). Some theoretical issues relating to educational evaluation. In R. W. Tyler (Ed.), *Educational evaluation. 68th yearbook of the National Society for the Study of Education, part 2* (pp. 26–50). Chicago, IL: University of Chicago Press.

Bloom, B. S., & Rakow, E. (1969). Higher mental processes. In R. L. Ebel (Ed.), *The encyclopedia of educational research, 4th edition.* New York, NY: Macmillan.

Bloom, B. S. (1970). Toward a theory of testing which includes measurement-evaluation-assessment. In M. C. Wittrock & D. E. Wiley (Eds.), *The evaluation of instruction.* New York, NY: Holt, Rinehart, & Winston.

Bloom, B. S. (1971a). *Individual differences in school achievement: A vanishing point?* Bloomington, IN: Phi Delta Kappan International.

Bloom, B. S. (1971b). Mastery learning. In J. H. Block (Ed.), *Mastery learning: Theory and practice* (pp. 47–63). New York, NY: Holt, Rinehart & Winston.

Bloom, B. S. (1971c). Affective consequences of school achievement. In J. H. Block (Ed.), *Mastery learning: Theory and practice* (pp. 13–28). New York, NY: Holt, Rinehart & Winston.

Bloom, B. S., Hastings, J. T., & Madaus, G. (1971). *Handbook on formative and summative evaluation of student learning*. New York, NY: McGraw-Hill.

Bloom, B. S. (1972). Innocence in education. *School Review, 80*(3), 332–352.

Bloom, B. S. (1973). Individual differences in school achievement: A vanishing point? In L. J. Rubin (Ed.), *Facts and feelings in the classroom*. New York, NY: Walker and Company.

Bloom, B. S. (1974a). Implications of the IEA studies for curriculum and instruction. *School Review, 82*(3), 413–435.

Bloom, B. S. (1974b). Time and learning. *American Psychologist, 29*(9), 682–688.

Bloom, B. S. (1974c). An introduction to mastery learning theory. In J. H. Block (Ed.), *Schools, society and mastery learning* (pp. 3–14). New York, NY: Holt, Rinehart & Winston.

Bloom, B. S. (1975). *Evaluation, instruction, and policy making*. IEP Seminar Paper No. 9. Paris, France: International Institute for Educational Planning, United Nations Educational, Scientific, and Cultural Organization (ERIC Document No. ED133855).

Bloom, B. S. (1976). *Human characteristics and school learning*. New York, NY: McGraw-Hill.

Bloom, B. S. (1977a). Affective outcomes of school learning. *Phi Delta Kappan, 59*(3), 193–198.

Bloom, B. S. (1977b). Favorable learning conditions for all. *Teacher, 95*(3), 22–28.

Bloom, B. S. (1977c). Only one-third of children learning. *Intellect, 106*(2390), 8–9.

Bloom, B. S. (Ed.) (1977d). *Research strategies for selected educational problems*. Chicago, IL: Department of Education, University of Chicago.

Bloom, B. S. (1978a). Changes in evaluation methods. In R. Glaser (Ed.) *Research and development and school change* (pp. 67–82). Hillsdale, NJ: Lawrence Erlbaum Associates.

Bloom, B. S. (1978b). New views of the learner: Implications for instruction and curriculum. *Educational Leadership, 35*(7), 563–571.

Bloom, B. S. (1979). New views of the learner: Implications for instruction and curriculum. *Childhood Education, 56*(1), 4–11.

Bloom, B. S. (1980a). The new direction in educational research: Alterable variables. *Phi Delta Kappan, 61*(6), 382–385.

Bloom, B. S. (1980b). The new direction in educational research: Alterable variables. *The Journal of Negro Education, 49*(3). 337–349.

Bloom, B. S. (1981a). *All our children learning: A primer for parents, teachers, and other educators*. New York, NY: McGraw-Hill.

Bloom, B. S. (1981b). Early learning in the home. In B. S. Bloom (Ed.), *All our children learning* (pp. 67–87). New York, NY: McGraw-Hill.

Bloom, B. S., Madaus, G. F., & Hastings, J. T. (1981). *Evaluation to improve learning*. New York. NY: McGraw-Hill.

Bloom, B. S., & Sosniak, L. A. (1981). Talent development vs. schooling. *Educational Leadership, 39*(2), 86–94.

Bloom, B. S. (1982a). The master teachers. *Phi Delta Kappan, 63*(10), 664–668, 715.

Bloom, B. S. (1982b). The role of gifts and markers in the development of talent. *Exceptional Children, 48*(6), 510–522.

Bloom, B. S. (1984a). The 2 sigma problem: The search for methods of group instruction as effective as one-to-one tutoring. *Educational Researcher, 13*(6), 4–16.

Bloom, B. S. (1984b). The search for methods of group instruction as effective as one-to-one tutoring. *Educational Leadership, 41*(8), 4–17.

Bloom, B. S. (Ed.) (1985). *Developing talent in young people.* New York, NY: Ballentine.

Bloom, B. S. (1986a). Automaticity: The hands and feet of genius. *Educational Leadership, 43*(5), 70–77.

Bloom, B. S. (1986b). The home environment and school learning. In Study Group on the National Assessment of Student Achievement (Ed.), *The nation's report card.* Washington, DC: Author (ERIC Document No. ED279663).

Bloom, B. S. (1986c). The international seminar for advanced training in curriculum development and innovation. In T. N. Postlethwaite (Ed.), *International educational research: Papers in honor of Torsten Husén* (pp. 145–162). Oxford, England: Pergamon Press.

Bloom, B. S. (1986d). What we're learning about teaching and learning: A summary of recent research. *Principal, 66*(2), 6–10.

Bloom, B. S. (1987). Response to Slavin's mastery learning reconsidered. *Review of Educational Research, 57*(4), 507–508.

Bloom, B. S. (1988a). Helping all children learn well in elementary school and beyond. *Principal, 67*(4), 12–17.

Bloom, B. S. (1988b). Ralph Tyler and the University of Chicago examination system. *Teaching Education, 2*(1), 47–53.

Bloom, B. S. (1988c). Response to Slavin: Toward a greater variety. *Educational Leadership, 46*(2), 28.

Kellaghan, T., Sloane, K., Alverez, B., & Bloom, B. S. (1993). *The home environment and school learning: Promoting parental involvement in the education of children.* San Francisco, CA: Jossey-Bass.

Bloom, B. S. (1994). Reflections on the development and use of the taxonomy. In L. W. Anderson & L. A. Sosniak (Eds.). *Bloom's taxonomy: A forty-year retrospective* (pp. 1–8). Chicago, IL: University of Chicago Press.

Appendix B
Writings about Benjamin S. Bloom and His Work

Calhoun, L. S. (1969). Chicago's Ben Bloom: All can learn. *Integrated Education*, 7(3), 16–20.

Sylwester, R. (1971). Benjamin Bloom and his taxonomy. *Instructor*, 80(6), 67–68.

Brandt, R. S. (1979). A conversation with Benjamin Bloom. *Educational Leadership*, 37(2), 157–161.

Cox, C. H. (1979). Basic skills through mastery learning: An interview with Benjamin S. Bloom, Part I. *Curriculum Review*, 18(5), 362–365.

Cox, C. H. (1980). Basic skills through mastery learning: An interview with Benjamin S. Bloom, Part II. *Curriculum Review*, 19(1), 10–14.

Hildebrand, J. (1980, July 15). Teaching "slow" students how to learn. *Newsday*, Part II, 2.

Alper, M. (1982). All our children can learn. *University of Chicago Magazine*, 74(4), 2–9, 30.

Brandt, R. S. (1985). On talent development: A conversation with Benjamin Bloom. *Educational Leadership*, 43(1), 33–35.

Guskey, T. R. (1985). Bloom's mastery learning: A legacy for effectiveness. *Educational Horizons*, 63(2), 90–92.

Koerner, T. F. (1986). A discussion about instruction and learning, teachers and schools: An interview with Benjamin S. Bloom. *NASSP Bulletin*, 70(493), 53–56, 58–59.

Safran, C. (1986). Go to the head of the class. *Reader's Digest*, December, 68–72.

Chance, P. (1987). Profile of Benjamin S. Bloom: Master of mastery. *Psychology Today*, 21(4), 42–46.

Anderson, L. W. (1988). Benjamin Bloom: His research and influence on education. *Teaching Education*, 2(1), 54–58.

Guskey, T. R. (1988). *Bloom's mastery learning and Hunter's mastery teaching: Complement or conflict?* Paper presented at the annual meeting of the American Educational Research Association, New Orleans, LA.

Marchant, G. J. (1991). The master educator: An interview with Benjamin S. Bloom. *Mid-Western Educational Researcher*, 4(1), 13–15.

Guskey, T. R. (1993). *Preservice and inservice professional development efforts regarding Bloom's Learning for Mastery.* Paper presented at the annual meeting of the American Educational Research Association, Atlanta, GA.

Guskey, T. R. (1994). Bloom's "Learning for Mastery" revisited: Modern perspectives and misinterpretations. *Outcomes, 13*(1), 16–39.

Anderson, L. W. (1996a). Benjamin Bloom, values and the professoriate. In C. Kridel, R. V. Bullough, Jr., & P. Shaker (Eds.), *Teachers and mentors: Profiles of distinguished twentieth-century professors of education* (pp. 45–54). New York, NY: Garland.

Anderson, L. W. (1996b). If you don't know who wrote it, you won't understand it: Lessons learned from Benjamin S. Bloom. *Peabody Journal of Education, 71*(1), 77–87.

Breslin, M. M. (1999, September 15). Benjamin Bloom, U. of C. prof who saw potential of all to learn. *Chicago Tribune*, Sec. 2, p. 11.

Davis, L. (Ed.) (1999, September). Bloom: Influential education researcher. *The University of Chicago Chronicle, 19*(1), 23.

Honan, W. H. (1999, September 13). Benjamin Bloom, 86, a leader in the creation of Head Start. *New York Times*, Sec. D, p. 2.

Savitz, F. (1999). *Howard Gardner, meet Benjamin Bloom: Strategies for the future enliven methods from the past.* Paper presented at the annual meeting of the Pennsylvania Council for the Social Studies, Pittsburgh, PA.

Woo, E. (1999, September 17). Benjamin S. Bloom; Education scholar's research influenced Head Start Program. *Los Angeles Times*, Sec. 4, p. 2.

Eisner, E. W. (2000). Benjamin Bloom, 1913–99. *Prospects: Quarterly Review of Comparative Education* (Issue 115), 30(3), 387–395 (ERIC Document No. ED448117).

Wolf, R. M. (2000). Benjamin S. Bloom. *IEA Newsletter, 26*, 1.

Anderson, L. W. (2001). *Benjamin S. Bloom 2001: The revised taxonomy as a tool for integrating learning, instruction, and assessment.* Paper presented at the annual meeting of the American Educational Research Association, Seattle, WA.

Guskey, T. R. (2001). *Benjamin S. Bloom's contributions to education and educational research.* Paper presented at the annual meeting of the American Educational Research Association, Seattle, WA.

Husén, T. (2001). Benjamin S. Bloom 1913–1999. In J. A. Palmer (Ed.), L. Bresler & D. E. Cooper (Assoc. Eds.), *Fifty modern thinkers in education: From Piaget to the present* (pp. 86–89). London, UK/New York, NY: Routledge.

Madaus, G. F. (2001). *Benjamin S. Bloom's contributions to testing, measurement, and evaluation.* Paper presented at the annual meeting of the American Educational Research Association, Seattle, WA.

Sosniak, L. (2001). *Benjamin S. Bloom and the development of talent.* Paper presented at the annual meeting of the American Educational Research Association, Seattle, WA.

Wolf, R. (2001). *Benjamin S. Bloom's contributions to international research and development.* Paper presented at the annual meeting of the American Educational Research Association, Seattle, WA.

154   *Appendix B*

Anderson, L. W. (2002). Benjamin Samuel Bloom (1913–1999). *American Psychologist, 57*(1), 63.

Anderson, L. W. (2003). Benjamin S. Bloom: His life, his works, his legacy. In B. J. Zimmermann & D. H. Schunk (Eds.), *Educational psychology: A century of contributions* (pp. 367–391). Mahwah, NJ: Erlbaum Associates.

Reedy, G. (2004). Benjamin S. Bloom. In A. Kovalchick & K. Dawson (eds.), *Education and technology: An encyclopedia, Vol. 1* (66–69). Santa Barbara, CA: ABC-Clio.

Guskey, T. R. (2005). Formative classroom assessment and Benjamin S. Bloom: Theory, research, and implications. *Man and Society, 57*(4), 219–233.

Guskey, T. R. (2007a). Formative classroom assessment and Benjamin S. Bloom: Theory, research, and practice. In J. H. McMillan (Ed.), *Formative Classroom Assessment: Theory into Practice* (pp. 63–78). New York, NY: Teachers College Press.

Guskey, T. R. (2007b). All our children learning: New views on the work of Benjamin S. Bloom. In A. M. Blankstein, R. W. Cole, & P. D. Houston (Eds.), *Ensuring High Achievement for Everybody's Children* (pp. 101–118). Thousand Oaks, CA: Corwin Press.

Guskey, T. R. (2007c). Closing achievement gaps: Revisiting Benjamin S. Bloom's "Learning for Mastery." *Journal of Advanced Academics, 19*(1), 8–31.

Guskey, T. R. (2010). Formative assessment: The contribution of Benjamin S. Bloom. In H. L. Andrade & G. J. Cizek (Eds.), *Handbook of Formative Assessment* (pp. 106–124). New York, NY: Routledge.

Appendix C
Doctoral Dissertation Students of Benjamin S. Bloom

Although best known for his work as a scholar and researcher, Ben's devotion to his students was unmatched. He served as the initial advisor to all students admitted to the Measurement, Evaluation, and Statistical Analysis (MESA) Program in the Department of Education at the University of Chicago. This meant that he was usually the first professor in the department that students met and the one who acquainted them with the MESA Program.

As their research interests became more focused, many students naturally moved away from Ben to work more closely with other professors in the department. But many others continued to work with him. Despite his reputation as a demanding taskmaster and his patent unwillingness to accept anything from students that was not their best work, the opportunity to experience firsthand his way of thinking and his unique way of approaching problems had amazing appeal to students.

Professors who direct the dissertation research of twenty-five or thirty students over the course of their academic careers are considered to have made a truly outstanding contribution. During his tenure at the University of Chicago, Ben chaired the doctoral dissertation committees of sixty-six students who graduated with Doctor of Philosophy degrees. He also served as a member of doctoral committees for sixty-nine additional students at the University of Chicago and a handful more during the latter part of his career at Northwestern University. The majority of these students went on to become professors at major universities throughout the United States and around the world, many having highly distinguished careers of their own. Below is a list of the doctoral students, listed chronologically by graduation date, whose dissertation research committees Ben chaired during his years at the University of Chicago.

Stella Beil Schulz, 1951
Ralph Goldner, 1952
  Tenafly, NJ
David Krathwohl, 1953
  Professor, Syracuse University, Syracuse, NY
Paul Ingraham Clifford, 1953
Earle George Eley, 1953
Emeliz Swain, 1953
Haron James Battle, 1954
Hymen Chausow, 1955
  Executive Vice Chancellor, City Colleges of Chicago, Chicago, IL
Sven Lundstedt, 1955
  Professor, Ohio State University, Columbus, OH
Frank Russell Peters, 1956
Gerard Allen Gladstein, 1957
  Professor, University of Rochester, Rochester, NY
Harry John LaPine, 1959
Barbara Grossman Berger, 1959
  Psychologist, New York City, NY
Moy Fook Gum, 1961
Elois Rachel Field, 1961
  Professor, University of Texas, Austin, TX
Douglas E. Stone, 1962
  Professor, University of South Florida, FL
William Bryan Dockrell, 1963
  Director, Scottish Council for Research in Education, Inveresk, Musselburgh, UK
Ravindrakumar H. Dave, 1963
Bom Mo Chung, 1964
  Professor, Seoul National University, Seoul, South Korea
Richard M. Wolf, 1964
  Professor, Teachers College, Columbia University, New York City, NY
Jagdish P. Dave, 1964
  Professor, Governors State University, University Park, IL
Izak DeVilliers Heyns, 1965
  Professor, University of Cape Town, Rondebosch, South Africa
Susan B. Stodolsky, 1965
  Professor, University of Chicago, Chicago, IL
Forest I. Harrison, 1967
  San Francisco, CA

Bobbie C. M. Anthony (Anthony-Perez), 1967
  Professor, Chicago State University, Chicago, IL
Jeremy D. Finn, 1967
  Professor, State University of New York at Buffalo, Buffalo, NY
Clarence Bradford, 1968
  Consultant, Los Angeles, CA
Hogwon Kim, 1968
  Professor, Yeungnam University, Kyungsan, South Korea
Peter Airasian, 1969
  Professor, Boston College, Chestnut Hill, MA
Christopher Modu, 1969
  Senior Statistical Associate, Educational Testing Service, Princeton, NJ
Joel Weiss, 1969
  Professor, Ontario Institute for Studies in Education, Toronto, Canada
James H. Block, 1970
  Professor, University of California, Santa Barbara, Santa Barbara, CA
Joung Kyu Whang, 1971
Ralph A. Hanson, 1972
  Consultant, Hanson Research Systems, Huntington Beach, CA
Szewach (Shevach) Eden, 1973
  Director of Curriculum Development, Ministry of Education and Culture, Jerusalem, Israel
Edward William Kifer, Jr., 1973
  Professor, University of Kentucky, Lexington, KY
Lorin Willard Anderson, 1973
  Professor, University of South Carolina, Columbia, SC
Wright Pearson, 1973
  Miami Lakes, FL
William Jerome Wright, 1973
Durmus Ali Ozcelik, 1974
  Professor, Anadolu Universites, Ankara, Turkey
Earnest A. Rakow, 1974
  Professor, University of Memphis, Memphis, TN
Tamar Levin, 1975
  Professor, University of Tel Aviv, Tel Aviv, Israel
Penny Edgert, 1975
  Sacramento, CA
Lawrence W. Hecht, 1977
  Senior Research Scientist, The College Board, Princeton, NJ
Guzver Yildiran, 1977
  Professor, Sisli, Istanbul, Turkey
Jong Seung Lee, 1978
  Professor, Chungnam National University, Daejon, South Korea

Thomas R. Guskey, 1979
   Professor, University of Kentucky, Lexington, KY
Abu Baker Nordin, 1979
Juan Enrique Froemel Andrarde, 1980
   Deputy Coordinator, Evaluation Laboratory, UNESCO-OREALC, Santiago, Chile
Lawrence Joseph Dolan, 1980
   Professor, Johns Hopkins University, Baltimore, MD
Zemira Mevarech, 1980
   Professor, University of Tel Aviv, Tel Aviv, Israel
Paul B. Duby, 1980
   Director, Office of Institutional Research and Planning, Northern Michigan University, Marquette, MI
John Q. Easton, 1981
   Director, Institute for Education Sciences, U.S. Department of Education, Washington, DC
Raymond E. Pifer, 1981
   Vice President, MARC, Greensboro, NC
Joanne Anania, 1981
   Professor, Roosevelt University, Chicago, IL
Gershon Tenenbaum, 1982
   Professor, Florida State University, Tallahassee, FL
Frank Guida, 1982
   Director of Program Evaluation & Research, Samaritan Village, Queens, NY
Fernando Leyton Soto, 1983
Arthur J. Burke, 1983
   Resource Coordinator, Vancouver Public Schools, Vancouver, WA
Suthan Janhom, 1984
   Professor, Chiang Mai University, Chiang Mai, Thailand
Eduardo Cabezon, 1984
   Professor, Universidad Metropolitana Ciencias Education, Santiago, Chile
George Engelhard, Jr., 1985
   Professor, Emory University, Atlanta, GA
Judith Ann Monsaas, 1985
   Professor, West Georgia College, Carrollton, GA
Kathryn D. Sloane, 1985
   Professor, University of Illinois at Urbana-Champaign, Champaign-Urbana, IL
Carlos A. Avalos-Valenzuela, 1986
   Director General, Universidad Leonardo da Vinci, Rancagua, Chile
Susanne Wegener Soled, 1986
   Professor, University of Cincinnati, Cincinnati, OH

Appendix D
Doctoral Dissertation Committees
of Benjamin S. Bloom

Below is a list of the sixty-nine doctoral students, listed chronologically by graduation date, on whose doctoral dissertation research committees Ben served as a member during his years at the University of Chicago.

Edward Furst, 1948
Pauline Margaret Alt, 1949
Hugh Victor Perkins, Jr., 1950
Frances Lucile Horler, 1950
Marvin Burack, 1951
Margaret Maurine Alexander, 1951
George Willett Hohl, 1952
Chalmer Gross, 1952
Egon G. Guba, 1953
Harry Bricker, 1953
James Mitchell, 1953
Lloyd Bernhard Urdal, 1954
Andrew Mathis, 1955
Douglas Johnson, 1955
Amy Frances Brown, 1955
Alexander Albert Liveright, 1955
Aubrey L. Ruess, 1956
Eldon Guy Wheeler, 1956
Walter Raine, 1956
Richard Chantry McVey,1957
John Jackson, 1957
Allen Bobroff, 1958

Nicholas Kushta, 1958
Myles Friedman, 1959
George Kenneth T. McGuire, 1959
Malcom Myers Provus, 1960
Jeanne Woolf, 1960
Kirpal Tijindar Singh, 1961
Willian James Hicklin, 1961
Roy John Ingham, 1962
Margaret A. Payne, 1963
Lee Shulman, 1963
Alexander Feldvebel, 1964
Khalil Ibrahi Al-Hamash, 1964
Carol Kehr Tittle, 1965
Barney M. Berlin, 1965
T. Josephy Sheehan, 1965
Arieh Lewy, 1966
Elizabeth Van de Roovaart, 1966
Gale Wood Roase, 1966
Anne Oliver Stemmler, 1967
Henriette Lahaderne, 1967
Daniel E. Lupto, 1967
William S. Hall, 1968
Harriet O'Brien, 1968
Ernest Jaski, 1969
Nargis Panchapakesan, 1969
William Marvin Bart, 1969
Arora Luigina Biamonte, 1969
Kay P. Torshen, 1969
John H. Buskey, 1970
Carita Chapman, 1971
Mildred Elizabeth Kersh, 1971
Dorothy Galbreath, 1972
Marshall Ney Arlin, Jr., 1973
Carlyle E. Maw, Jr., 1979
Edward D. Haertel, 1980
Geoff Norman Masters, 1981
Ann Stephanie Stano, 1981
Lauren A. Sosniak, 1983
Jan Carol Naslund, 1987
William Coleman Gustin, 1987
E. Mathew Schul, 1988
Robert Chares Frosh, 1988
Dorthea Juul, 1989

Lih-Meei Yang, 1989
Carol Monroe Myford, 1989
Raul Jesus Enrique Pizarro Sanchez, 1991
Myong Sook Kim, 1991

References
Works Other Than Those of Benjamin S. Bloom

Adelman, C. (1999). *Answers in the tool box: Academic intensity, attendance patterns, and bachelor's degree attainment.* Washington, DC: Office of Educational Research and Improvement, U.S. Department of Education.

Aikin, W. (1942). *Adventure in American education, Vol. 1: Story of the Eight-Year Study.* New York, NY: Harper & Brothers.

Ambrose, S. A., Bridges, M. W., DiPietro, M., Lovett, M. C., & Norman, M. K. (2010). *How learning works: Seven research-based principles for smart teaching.* San Francisco, CA: Jossey-Bass.

Anania, J. (1981). *The effects of quality of instruction on the cognitive and affective learning of students.* Unpublished doctoral dissertation, University of Chicago, Chicago, IL.

Anania, J. (1983). The influence of instructional conditions on student learning and achievement. *Evaluation in Education: An International Review Series, 7*(1), 1–92.

Anderson, L. W. (1994). Research on teaching and teacher education. In L. W. Anderson & L. A. Sosniak (Eds.). *Bloom's taxonomy: A forty-year retrospective* (pp. 126–145). Chicago. IL: University of Chicago Press.

Anderson, L. W., & Krathwohl, D. R. (Eds.) (2001). *A taxonomy for learning, teaching, and assessing: A revision of Bloom's taxonomy of educational objectives.* New York, NY: Longman.

Anderson, L. W., & Sosniak, L. A. (Eds.). (1994). *Bloom's taxonomy: A forty-year retrospective.* Chicago, IL: University of Chicago Press.

Anderson, S. A. (1994a). Staff development and implementation of mastery learning: A field study. *Outcomes, 13*(2), 12–20.

Anderson, S. A. (1994b). *Synthesis of research on mastery learning.* Washington, DC: National Educational Association (ERIC Document Reproduction Service No. ED382567).

Arends, R. I., & Kilcher, A. (2010). *Teaching for student learning: Becoming an accomplished teacher.* New York, NY: Routledge.

164   *References*

Benjamin, R. (1981). All kids can learn: Mastery learning. Chapter 2 in *Making schools work*. New York, NY: Continuum.

Beyer, B. K. (2008). What research tells us about teaching thinking skills. *The Social Studies*, 99(5), 223–232.

Blank, R. K. (2011). *Closing the achievement gap for economically disadvantaged students? Analyzing change since No Child Left Behind using state assessments and the National Assessment of Educational Progress*. Washington, DC: Council of Chief State School Officers.

Block, J. H. (Ed.). (1971). *Mastery learning: Theory and practice*. New York, NY: Holt, Rinehart & Winston.

Block, J. H. (Ed.) (1974). *Schools, society and mastery learning*. New York, NY: Holt, Rinehart & Winston.

Block, J. H., & Anderson, L. W. (1975). *Mastery learning in classroom instruction*. New York, NY: Macmillan.

Block, J. H., & Burns, R. B. (1976). Mastery learning. In L. S. Shulman (Ed.), *Review of research in education* (Vol. 4, pp. 3–49). Itasca, IL: Peacock.

Bloom, S. (1976). *Peer and cross-age tutoring in the schools*. Washington, DC: National Institute of Education.

Bruner, J. S. (1992). Another look at new look 1. *American Psychologist*, 47(6), 780–783.

Burke, A. J. (1983). *Students' potential for learning contrasted under tutorial and group approaches to instruction*. Unpublished doctoral dissertation, University of Chicago, Chicago, IL.

Burns, R. B. (1986). Accumulating the accumulated evidence on mastery learning. *Outcomes*, 5(2), 4–10.

Cabezon, E. (1984). *The effects of marked changes in student achievement patterns on the students, their teachers, and their parents: The Chilean case*. Unpublished doctoral dissertation, University of Chicago, Chicago, IL.

Carroll, J. (1963). A model for school learning. *Teachers College Record*, 64, 723–733.

Chan, K. S. (1981). *The interaction of aptitude with mastery versus non-mastery instruction: Effects on reading comprehension of grade three students*. Unpublished doctoral dissertation, University of Western Australia, Perth, Australia.

Chance, P. (1987). Profile of Benjamin S. Bloom: Master of mastery. *Psychology Today*, 21(4), 42–46.

Chung, B. M. (1994). The Taxonomy in the Republic of Korea. In L. W. Anderson & L. A. Sosniak (Eds.), *Bloom's taxonomy: A forty-year retrospective* (pp. 164–173). Chicago, IL: University of Chicago Press.

Coleman, J. S., Campbell, E., Hobson, C., McPartland, J., Mood, A., Weinfield, R., & York, R. (1966). *Equality of educational opportunity*. Washington, DC: U.S. Government Printing Office.

Creech, A., & Hallam, S. (2011). Learning a musical instrument: The influence of interpersonal interaction on outcomes for school-aged pupils. *Psychology of Music*, 39(1), 102–122.

Dollard, J., & Miller, N. E. (1950). *Personality and psychotherapy*. New York, NY: McGraw-Hill.

Dyke, W. E. (1988). *The immediate effect of a mastery learning program on the belief systems of high school teachers*. Paper presented at the annual meeting of the American Educational Research Association, New Orleans, LA.

Eby, J. (1983). Gifted behavior: A non-elitist approach. *Educational Leadership, 40*(8), 30–36.

Eby, J. (1984). Developing gifted behavior. *Educational Leadership, 41*(7), 35–43.

Ellis, A. K., & Fouts, J. T. (1993). *Research on educational innovations*. Princeton Junction, NJ: Eye on Education, Inc.

Fiske, E. B. (1980, March 30). New teaching method produces impressive gains. *New York Times*, pp. 1, 37.

Furst, E. J. (1994). Bloom's taxonomy: Philosophical and educational issues. In L. W. Anderson & L. A. Sosniak (Eds.), *Bloom's taxonomy: A forty-year retrospective* (pp. 28–40). Chicago, IL: University of Chicago Press.

Gilbert, W., & Hamel, T. (2011). Enhancing coach-parent relationships in youth sports: Increasing harmony and minimizing hassle. *International Journal of Sports Science and Coaching, 6*(1), 37–42.

Glaser, R. (1966). *The program for individually prescribed instruction*. Pittsburgh, PA: University of Pittsburgh.

Good, T. L. (1983). Research on classroom teaching. In L. S. Shulman & G. Sykes (Eds.), *Handbook of teaching and policy* (pp. 42–80). New York, NY: Longman.

Guskey, T. R. (1985). *Implementing mastery learning*. Belmont, CA: Wadsworth.

Guskey, T. R. (1997). *Implementing mastery learning* (2nd ed.). Belmont, CA: Wadsworth.

Guskey, T. R. (2005). A historical perspective on closing achievement gaps. *NASSP Bulletin, 89*(644), 76–89.

Guskey, T. R. (2007). Closing achievement gaps: Revisiting Benjamin S. Bloom's "Learning for Mastery." *Journal of Advanced Academics, 19*(1), 8–31.

Guskey, T. R. (2009a). Mastery learning. In E. M. Anderman & L. H. Anderman (Eds.), *Psychology of Classroom Learning: An Encyclopedia.*(Vol. II, pp. 585–91). Detroit, MI: Macmillan Reference USA.

Guskey, T. R. (2009b). Mastery learning. In T. L. Good (Ed.), *21st Century Education: A Reference Handbook* (Vol. I, pp. 194–202).Thousand Oaks, CA: Sage Publications.

Guskey, T. R. (2010). Lessons of mastery learning. *Educational Leadership, 68*(2), 52–57.

Guskey, T. R., & Gates, S. (1986). Synthesis of research on the effects of mastery learning in elementary and secondary classrooms. *Educational Leadership, 45*(8), 73–80.

Guskey, T. R., & Pigott, T. D. (1988). Research on group-based mastery learning programs: A meta-analysis. *Journal of Educational Research, 81*(4), 197–216.

Hardman, M. L., Drew, C. J., & Egan, W. (2010). *Human exceptionality: School, community, and family* (10th ed.). Belmont, CA: Wadsworth, Cengage Learning.

Hattie, J. (2009). *Visible learning: A synthesis of over 800 meta-analyses relating to achievement*. New York, NY: Routledge.

Hau-sut, H. (1990). *A study of mastery learning and its effects on science achievement, retention, attitudes, and self-concepts with special focus on educationally disadvantaged students*. Master's thesis, Chinese University of Hong Kong, Hong Kong SAR, The People's Republic of China.

Honan, W. H. (1999, September 13). Benjamin Bloom, 86, a leader in the creation of Head Start. *New York Times*.

Jeffrey, L. M., Hide, S., & Lett, S. (2010). Learning characteristics of small business managers: Principles for training. *Journal of Workplace Learning, 22*(3), 146–165.

Kagan, N., Krathwohl, D., & Miller, R. M. (1963). Stimulated recall in therapy using videotape: A case study. *Journal of Counseling Psychology, 10*(3), 237–243.

Karch, A. (2010). Policy feedback and preschool finding in the American states. *Policy Studies Journal, 38*(2), 217–234.

Kilgore, S. B., & Reynolds, K. J. (2011). *From silos to success: Reframing schools for success.* Thousand Oaks, CA: Corwin Press.

Kim, H., et al. (1969). *A study of the Bloom strategies for mastery learning.* Seoul, Korea: Korean Institute for Research in the Behavioral Sciences (in Korean).

Kim, H., et al. (1970). *The Mastery Learning Project in the middle schools.* Seoul, Korea: Korean Institute for Research in the Behavioral Sciences (in Korean).

Klausmeier, H. J. (1971). The multi-unit elementary school and individually guided education. *Phi Delta Kappan, 53*(3), 181–184.

Klausmeier, H. J., et al. (1968). *Individually guided education in the multi-unit school: Guidelines for implementation.* Washington, DC: Office of Education (DHEW), Bureau of Research.

Koenig, R. (2010). *Learning for keeps: Teaching the strategies essential for creating independent learners.* Alexandria, VA: Association for Supervision and Curriculum Development.

Krathwohl, D. R. (1994). Reflections on the taxonomy: Its past, present, and future. In L. W. Anderson & L. A. Sosniak (Eds.), *Bloom's taxonomy: A forty-year retrospective* (pp. 181–202). Chicago, IL: University of Chicago Press.

Kulik, C. C., Kulik, J. A., & Bangert-Drowns, R. L. (1990). Effectiveness of mastery learning programs: A meta-analysis. *Review of Educational Research, 60*(2), 265–299.

Kulik, J. A., & Kulik, C. C. (1989). Meta-analysis in education. *International Journal of Educational Research, 13*, 221–340.

Langeheine, R. (1992). *State mastery learning: Dynamic models for longitudinal data.* Paper presented at the annual meeting of the American Educational Research Association, San Francisco, CA.

Levin, T. (1979). Instruction which enables students to develop of higher mental processes. *Evaluation in Education: An International Review Series, 3*(3), 173–220.

Lewy, A., & Báthory, Z. (1994). The *taxonomy of educational objectives* in continental Europe, the Mediterranean, and the Middle East. In L. W. Anderson & L. A. Sosniak (Eds.), *Bloom's taxonomy: A forty-year retrospective* (pp. 146–163). Chicago, IL: University of Chicago Press.

Leyton, F. S. (1983). *The extent to which group instruction supplemented by mastery of initial cognitive prerequisites approximates the learning effectiveness of one-to-one tutorial methods.* Unpublished doctoral dissertation, University of Chicago, Chicago, IL.

Marzano, R. J. (2001). *Designing a new taxonomy of educational objectives.* Thousand Oaks, CA: Corwin.

Marzano, R. J., Frontier, T., & Livingston, D. (2011). *Effective supervision: Supporting the art and science of teaching.* Alexandria, VA: Association for Supervision and Curriculum Development.

Mevarech, Z. R. (1980). *The role of teaching learning strategies and feedback-corrective procedures in developing higher cognitive achievement.* Unpublished doctoral dissertation, University of Chicago, Chicago, IL.

Mevarech, Z. R. (1985). The effects of cooperative mastery learning strategies on mathematical achievement. *Journal of Educational Research, 78*(6), 372–377.

Mevarech, Z. R. (1986). The role of a feedback-corrective procedure in developing mathematics achievement and self-concept in desegregated classrooms. *Studies in Educational Evaluation, 12,* 197–203.

Miller, D. F. (2010). *Positive child guidance* (6th ed.). Belmont, CA: Wadsworth, Cengage Learning.

Morawska, A., & Sanders, M. R. (2009). Parenting gifted and talented children: Conceptual and empirical foundations. *Gifted Child Quarterly, 53*(3), 163–173.

Morrison, H. C. (1926). *The practice of teaching in the secondary school.* Chicago, IL: University of Chicago Press.

Morrow, J. R., Jackson, J. W., Disch, J. G., & Mood, D. P. (2010). *Measurement and evaluation in human performance* (4th ed.). Champaign, IL: Human Kinetics.

Newman, H. H., Freeman, F. N., & Holzinger, K. J. (1937). *Twins: A study of heredity and environment.* Chicago, IL: University of Chicago Press.

Nickerson, R. S. (2010). *Mathematical reasoning: Patterns, problems, conjectures, and proofs.* New York, NY: Psychology Press, Taylor & Francis Group.

Nordin, A. B. (1979). *The effects of different qualities of instruction on selected cognitive, affective, and time variables.* Unpublished doctoral dissertation, University of Chicago, Chicago, IL.

Novak, J. D. (2010). *Learning, creating, and using knowledge: Concept maps as facilitative tools in schools and corporations* (2nd ed.). New York, NY: Routledge.

Phillips, D. A., & Lowenstein, A. E. (2011). Early care, education, and child development. *Annual Review of Psychology, 62,* 483–500.

Platt, J. R. (1964). Strong inference. *Science, 146*(3), 347–353.

Postlethwaite, T. N. (1994). Validity vs. utility: Personal experiences with the Taxonomy. In L. W. Anderson & L. A. Sosniak (Eds.), *Bloom's taxonomy: A forty-year retrospective* (pp. 174–180). Chicago, IL: University of Chicago Press.

Powell, R. G., & Powell, D. L. (2010). *Classroom communication and diversity: Enhancing instructional practice* (2nd ed.). New York, NY: Routledge.

Reezigt, B. J., & Weide, M. G. (1990). *The effects of group-based mastery learning on language and arithmetic achievement and attitudes in primary education in the Netherlands.* Paper presented at the annual meeting of the American Educational Research Association, Boston, MA.

Reezigt, G. J., & Weide, M. G. (1992). *Mastery learning and instructional effectiveness.* Paper presented at the annual meeting of the American Educational Research Association, San Francisco, CA.

Richardson, M. W. & Kuder, C. F. (1939). The calculation of test reliability coefficients based on the method of rational equivalence. *Journal of Educational Psychology, 31*(4), 681–687.

Richardson, M. W., Russell, J. T., Snalnaker, J. M., & Thurstone, L. L. (1933). *Manual of examination methods.* Chicago, IL: University of Chicago Board of Examinations.

Scanlon, R. G. (1966). *Individually prescribed instruction: A manual for the IPI institute.* Washington, DC: Office of Education (DHEW), Bureau of Research.

Smith, E. R., & Tyler, R. W. (1942). *Appraising and recording student progress.* New York, NY: Harper & Brothers.

Snalnaker, J. M. (1934). The construction and results of a twelve-hour test in English composition. *School and Society, 39*(2), 193–198.

Sosniak, L. A. (1994). The *Taxonomy*, curriculum, and their relations. In L. W. Anderson & L. A. Sosniak (Eds.), *Bloom's taxonomy: A forty-year retrospective* (pp. 103–125). Chicago, IL: University of Chicago Press.

Sosniak, L. A. (2001). *Benjamin S. Bloom and the development of talent.* Paper presented at the annual meeting of the American Educational Research Association, Seattle, WA.

Starko, A. J. (2010). *Creativity in the classroom: Schools of curious delight* (4th ed.). New York, NY: Routledge.

Stenning, K., & van Lambalgen, M. (2008). *Human reasoning and cognitive science.* Cambridge, MA: Massachusetts Institute of Technology Press.

Sternberg, R. J., Jarvin, L., & Grigorenko, E. L. (2011). *Explorations in giftedness.* New York, NY: Cambridge University Press.

Tenenbaum, G. (1982). *A method of group instruction which is as effective as one-to-one tutorial instruction.* Unpublished doctoral dissertation, University of Chicago, Chicago, IL.

Thorndike, R. L., & Hagen, E. P. (1969). *Measurement and evaluation in psychology and education* (3rd ed.). Englewood Cliffs, NJ: Prentice Hall.

Thurstone, L. L. (1937). *Manual of examination methods* (2nd ed.). Chicago, IL: University of Chicago Press.

Tyler, R. W. (1942). General statement on evaluation. *Journal of Educational Research, 35*(4), 492–501.

Tyler, R. W. (1949). *Basic principles of curriculum and instruction.* Chicago, IL: University of Chicago Press.

U.S. Congress. (2001). *No Child Left Behind Act of 2001.*

Vickery, T. R. (1987). *Evaluating a mastery learning high school.* Paper presented at the annual meeting of the American Educational Research Association, Washington, DC.

Waddington, T. (1995). *Why mastery matters.* Paper presented at the annual meeting of the American Educational Research Association, San Francisco, CA.

Walberg, H. J. (1984). Improving the productivity of America's schools. *Educational Leadership, 41*(8), 19–27.

Washburne, C. W. (1922). Educational measurements as a key to individualizing instruction and promotions. *Journal of Educational Research, 5*, 195–206.

Wiggins, G., & McTighe, J. (2011). *The understanding by design guide to creating high quality units.* Alexandria, VA: Association for Supervision and Curriculum Development.

Wiliam, D. (2010). An integrative summary of the research literature and implications for a new theory of formative assessment. In H. L. Andrade & G. J. Cizek (Eds.), *Handbook of Formative Assessment* (pp. 18–40). New York, NY: Routledge.

Woo, E. (1999, September 17). Benjamin S. Bloom; Education scholar's research influenced Head Start program. *Los Angeles Times.*

Wu, W. Y. (1994). *Mastery learning in Hong Kong: Challenges and prospects.* Paper presented at the annual meeting of the American Educational Research Association, New Orleans, LA.

About the Contributors

Those who responded to my request in 2004 offered many wonderful and touching stories. Others wrote back saying they had no special stories to share but wished me well with the project and looked forward to the resulting publication. While I was not able to include all of the stories I received, I am deeply indebted to the following individuals for their kind responses. Each person is listed with their professional affiliation at the time of their response in 2004:

Peter W. Airasian, Professor of Education, Boston College, Chestnut Hill, MA

Joanne Anania, Professor of Education, Roosevelt University, Chicago, IL

Lorin W. Anderson, Professor of Education, University of South Carolina, Columbia, SC

Bobbie M. Anthony-Perez, Professor Emeritus of Psychology, Chicago State University, Chicago, IL

Barbara G. Berger, Psychologist and Psychotherapist, Mental Health Clinic, New York City, NY

Charles Bidwell, Professor of Education, University of Chicago, Chicago, IL

James H. Block, Professor of Education, University of California at Santa Barbara, Santa Barbara, CA

Hymen M. Chausow, Executive Vice Chancellor of Academic Affairs Emeritus, City Colleges of Chicago, Chicago, IL

Robert Dreeben, Professor of Education Emeritus, University of Chicago, Chicago, IL

Judy Eby, Director of Gifted Education, San Diego, CA

Shevach Eden, Director of the Israeli Curriculum Center (retired), Chairman of the Pedagogical Secretariat, Ministry of Education, Jerusalem, Israel

Elliot W. Eisner, Lee Jacks Professor of Education and Professor of Art, Stanford University, Stanford, CA

George Engelhard, Jr., Professor of Educational Studies, Emory University, Atlanta, GA

Elois R. Field, Professor of Education (retired), University of Texas at Arlington, Arlington, TX

Jeremy D. Finn, Professor of Education, State University of New York at Buffalo, Buffalo, NY

Juan E. Froemel, Deputy Coordinator, Latin American Laboratory for Assessment of Quality in Education, UNESCO-OREALC, Santiago, Chile

Jacob Getzels, Professor of Education Emeritus, University of Chicago, Chicago, IL

John I. Goodlad, President, Institute for Educational Inquiry, Seattle, WA

Frank V. Guida, Director of Research and Program Evaluation, Samaritan Village, Inc., Briarwood, NY

Torsten Husén, Professor Emeritus, Stockholm University, Royal Swedish Academy of Sciences, Stockholm, Sweden

Edward (Skip) Kifer, Professor of Education, University of Kentucky, Lexington, KY

David R. Krathwohl, Hannah Hammond Professor of Education Emeritus, Syracuse University, Syracuse, NY

Frederick F. Lighthall, Professor of Education, University of Chicago, Chicago, IL

Christopher C. Modu, Chief-of-Party, Technical Assistance Team, World Bank Education Project, Liberia; Associate Director (retired), Statistical Analysis Division, Educational Testing Service, Princeton, NJ

Judith A. Monsaas, Director of P-16 Assessment and Evaluation, Board of Regents of the University System of Georgia, Atlanta, GA

Akio Nakajima, President, Japan Educational Exchange, Baba Foundation, Tokyo, Japan

Roy W. Phillips, Past Executive Director of IEA, Assistant Director (retired), Curriculum Development Division, Department of Education, Queenstown, New Zealand

T. Neville Postlethwaite, Professor Emeritus, University of Hamburg, Baigts-de-Béarn, France

Leah Shefatya, Henrietta Szold Institute (retired), Jerusalem, Israel

Lee S. Shulman, President, The Carnegie Foundation for the Advancement of Teaching; Charles E. Ducommun Professor of Education Emeritus, Stanford University, Stanford, CA

Jeffrey K. Smith, Professor, College of Education, University of Otago, Dunedin, New Zealand

Suzanne Wegener Soled, Associate Professor of Education, University of Cincinnati, Cincinnati, OH

Lauren Sosniak, Professor of Education, San Jose State University, San Jose, CA

Gershon Tenenbaum, Professor of Sport and Exercise Psychology, Florida State University, Tallahassee, FL

Zalman Usiskin, Professor of Education, Director, School Mathematics Project, University of Chicago, Chicago, IL

Richard M. Wolf, Professor Emeritus of Education and Psychology, Columbia University, New York, NY